Science Fiction Films

www.pocketessentials.com

Other Books in this series by the same author

David Cronenberg
Writing a Screenplay

Science Fiction Films

John Costello

www.pocketessentials.com

FILM
PN
1995.9
.S26
C678
2003

This edition published in 2004 by Pocket Essentials,
P.O. Box 394, Harpenden, Herts,AL5 1JX

Distributed in the USA by Trafalgar Square Publishing, PO Box 257, Howe Hill
Road, North Pomfret,Vermont 05053

http://www.pocketessentials.com

Copyright © John Costello 2004

The right of John Costello to be identified as the author of this work has been asserted by
him in accordance with the Copyright, Designs and Patents Act 1988.

All rights reserved. No part of this book may be reproduced, stored in or introduced into a
retrieval system, or transmitted, in any form, or by any means (electronic, mechanical,
photocopying, recording or otherwise) without the written permission
of the publisher. Any person who does any unauthorised act in relation to this
publication may be liable to criminal prosecution and civil claims for damages.The book is
sold subject to the condition that it shall not, by way of trade or otherwise, be lent, re-sold,
hired out or otherwise circulated, without the publisher's prior consent, in any form or
binding or cover other than in which it is published, and without similar conditions,
including this condition being imposed on the subsequent publication.

A CIP catalogue record for this book is available from the British Library.

ISBN 1 903047 44 7

9 8 7 6 5 4 3 2 1

Book typeset by Avocet Typeset, Chilton, Aylesbury, Bucks
Printed and bound in Great Britain by Cox & Wyman, Reading, Berks

'...while the world moves
In appetency, on its metalled ways
Of time past and time future.'
T.S. Eliot, from 'Burnt Norton'

'Science friction burns my fingers.'
XTC

'We are the Robots.'
Kraftwerk, 'The Robots', from the album *The Man Machine*

Dedication

With love to Dad, 1926–2002, who never liked science fiction but would have liked this because I wrote it; and to Mum, who also never liked sf but will be chuffed with the dedication; and to my wife Michelle, to whom I couldn't be more dedicated.

Acknowledgements

Thanks to Michelle for putting up with the long alien gestation period and forgoing a holiday in the South of France; Simon Maddocks for useful contributions; Dave Bullivant for consistent, contrary positions on *Solaris* and Spielberg; and the late, great Philip K. Dick for the many abuses his work has suffered en route to the big screen.

Accompaniments

Cabaret Voltaire, Clock DVA, DAF, Data, Devo, Eno, Fad Gadget, The Faint, John Foxx, Goldfrapp, Beaumont Hannant, Hard Corps, The Human League, Japan, Jean-Michel Jarre, Kraftwerk, Liaisons Dangereuses, The Metronomes, Minny Pops, The Names, Gary Numan, OMD, Portion Control, Propaganda, Recoil, The Residents, Klaus Schulze, Severed Heads, Soft Cell, Synergy, Bernard Szajner, Tangerine Dream, Rolf Trostel, Tuxedomoon, Vangelis, Vice Versa, Wall Of Voodoo, Wire, Yello, Yellow Magic Orchestra

Contents

10: We Have Ignition: Introduction   9

9: The Future As It Was Yesterday (1900–1936)   17
Le Voyage Dans La Lune [A Trip To The Moon] (1902), Paris Qui Dort [aka The Crazy Ray] (1923), Aelita (1924), Metropolis (1926), Things To Come (1936)

8: Fear Is The Key (1950–1959)   24
Destination Moon (1950), When Worlds Collide (1951), This Island Earth (1955), FORBIDDEN PLANET (1956), The Thing [aka The Thing From Another World] (1951), THE DAY THE EARTH STOOD STILL (1951), The War Of The Worlds (1953), It Came From Outer Space (1953), Invaders From Mars (1953), The Quatermass Xperiment [aka The Creeping Unknown] (1955), Earth Vs. The Flying Saucers (1956), INVASION OF THE BODY SNATCHERS (1956), The Incredible Shrinking Man (1957), I Married A Monster From Outer Space (1958), On The Beach (1959)

7: Damned Strange Odysseys (1960–1968)   44
The Time Machine (1960), La Jetée (1962), Dr. Strangelove Or: How I Learned To Stop Worrying And Love The Bomb (1963), Alphaville: Une Étrange Aventure De Lemmy Caution (1965), Daleks – Invasion Earth 2150 A.D. (1966), Fahrenheit 451 (1966), Fantastic Voyage (1966), Barbarella (1968), Charly (1968), Planet Of The Apes (1968), 2001: A SPACE ODYSSEY (1968)

6: Dystopia, Dattopia (1970–1976)   55
The Andromeda Strain (1970), THX 1138 (1970), A Clockwork Orange (1971), Slaughterhouse Five (1971), Silent Running (1972), Solaris [Solyaris] (1972), Sleeper (1973), Westworld (1973), Soylent Green (1973), DARK STAR (1974), Rollerball (1975), A Boy And His Dog (1975), The Man Who Fell To Earth (1976)

5: The Biggest Bang (1977–1982)   69
Star Wars Episode IV: A New Hope (1977), Close Encounters Of The Third Kind (1977), Demon Seed (1977), Invasion Of The Body Snatchers (1978), ALIEN (1979), Mad Max (1979), Star Trek: The Motion Picture (1979), Altered States (1980), Scanners (1980), The

Empire Strikes Back [Star Wars Episode V] (1980), Escape From New York (1981), MAD MAX 2 [aka The Road Warrior] (1981), Outland (1981), BLADE RUNNER (1982), THE THING (1982), E.T. The Extra-Terrestrial (1982), Videodrome (1982), Tron (1982), Star Trek II: The Wrath Of Khan (1982), Android (1982), Liquid Sky (1982)

4: Post-Bang Boom (1983–1989)   98
Return Of The Jedi [Star Wars Episode VI] (1983), The Last Battle [Le Dernier Combat] (1983), Koyaanisqatsi (1983), THE TERMINATOR (1984), 2010: The Year We Make Contact (1984), Dune (1984), Starman (1984), Back To The Future (1985), Brazil (1985), Lifeforce (1985), The Fly (1986), Aliens (1986), Robocop (1987), Predator (1987), The Hidden (1988), They Live (1988), Miracle Mile (1988), The Abyss (1989)

3: Fin De Siècle (1990–1999)   116
Total Recall (1990), Terminator 2: Judgment Day (1991), Until The End Of The World [Bis Ans Ende Der Welt] (1991), Jurassic Park (1993), Johnny Mnemonic (1995), Strange Days (1995), 12 Monkeys (1995), Mars Attacks! (1996), Space Truckers (1996), Contact (1997), Cube (1997), The Fifth Element [Le Cinquième Elément] (1997), Men In Black (1997), Gattaca (1997), Starship Troopers (1997), Open Your Eyes [Abre Los Ojos] (1997), Last Night (1998), The Matrix (1999), eXistenZ (1999)

2: New Millennium, Old Stories (2000–2003)   132
The Cell (2000), Pitch Black (2000), Avalon (2001), Minority Report (2002), Cypher (2002), Terminator 3: Rise Of The Machines (2003)

1: 2-D Or Beyond 2-D: Animations   138
Fantastic Planet [La Planète Sauvage] (1973), Heavy Metal (1981), When The Wind Blows (1986), Akira (1988), Ghost In The Shell [Kokaku Kidotai] (1995), The Iron Giant (1999), Final Fantasy: The Spirits Within (2001)

0: ZEROS: Exploded On The Launch Pad   145
Robot Monster (1953), Plan 9 From Outer Space (1956), Zardoz (1973), Logan's Run (1976), The Black Hole (1979), Flash Gordon (1980), Waterworld (1995), Screamers (1995), Independence Day [aka ID4] (1996), Event Horizon (1997), Lost In Space (1998), Battlefield: Earth (2000), Mission To Mars (2000), Ghosts Of Mars (2001), Planet Of The Apes (2001), A.I. Artificial Intelligence (2001)

−1: Afterword: The New Dystopia?   156

References And Notes   158

10: We Have Ignition: Introduction

'The real world is much more frightening than any alien planet that anyone's ever going to dream up.'
William Gibson (author/screenwriter)

Sense Of Wonder

Washington DC, 1951: A humanoid figure and a giant robot emerge from the first alien spaceship to land on Earth. The humanoid raises its hand. In the surrounding army cordon a nervous young soldier aims his rifle and fires.

Los Angeles, 2019: As his life ebbs away in genetically programmed termination, an android 'Replicant' delivers a lesson in humanity to his human nemesis whose life he has just spared.

Antarctica, 1982: The two survivors of an attack on a US research station by a shapeshifting alien lifeform face the prospect of freezing to death together, neither certain that the other is really human.

Altair IV, 2200: While the crew of the space cruiser C57–D sleeps, something huge, invisible and *very* angry tears its way through the perimeter force field.

Earth, The Dawn Of Man: In the shadow of a colossal black alien monolith, an early hominid kills a rival with an animal bone, setting mankind on the road to conquering the planet and reaching out into the Solar System.

These scenes, from *The Day The Earth Stood Still*, *Blade Runner*, *The Thing*, *Forbidden Planet* and *2001: A Space Odyssey*, showcase the science fiction genre at its most original, dynamic and thought-provoking. Unfortunately, the public perception of sf cinema (please, never use 'sci-fi' – I'll explain why shortly) tends toward giant insects, silver jockstraps and po-faced aliens with radio antennae. Most commentators would probably include four of the above five movies in their top ten, with the exception of *The Thing*; however, they'd probably include *The Thing From Another World*. More than most genres, a handful of classic sf movies stand head and shoulders above the rest, yet sf movies remain enduringly popular. This book looks at a selection of the great, the not so great and the downright awful – as I see them. That may be through lenses rose-tinted, cracked or opaque, but they're mine. While searching for a way to describe my relationship with sf movies, I realised Bill Warren's intro to his book *Keep Watching The Skies!* said it for me: 'This is an *intensely* personal book ... This book is not a history; it's not a survey; it's a personal report ... I'm writing the book because I feel that my affection for the genre has permitted me certain insights into the movies as individual films and as part of a phenomenon.'

Of course, I'm only scratching the surface. Lucky old Bill had 1,300 pages on sf movies from 1950 to 1962 alone. There are many films I wish I'd had space to include, and many others I'd like to have covered in more depth. I've omitted 'monster movies', 'disaster movies' and 'comic superheroes' because such subgenres are not strictly sf, although even that assumption is problematic.

Genre: Science Fiction

The one thing upon which sf practitioners and critics agree is the fruitlessness of trying to define the genre, so I won't attempt to. Instead, I'll turn to the thoughts of a couple of luminaries, firstly my favourite sf author, Philip K Dick: 'We have a fictitious world; that is the first step: it is a society that does not in fact exist, but is predicated on our known society; that is, our known society acts as a jumping-off point for it ... It is our world ... transformed into that which it is not or not yet. This world must differ from the given in at least one way ... to give rise to events that could not occur in our society ... There must be a coherent idea involved in this dislocation;

that is, the dislocation must be a conceptual one, not merely a trivial or bizarre one – *this* is the essence of science fiction ... *the shock of dysrecognition* ... I think Dr Willis McNelly at the California State University at Fullerton put it best when he said that the true protagonist of an sf story or novel is an idea and not a person.'

Author and sf aficionado Kingsley Amis acknowledged the magnetic appeal of sf in his 1960 survey of sf literature, *New Maps Of Hell*: 'Those who decide that they ought to "find out about" science fiction, suspecting that it furnishes a new vantage point from which to survey "our culture", will find much to confirm that suspicion and also, I hope, much incidental entertainment, but they are unlikely to be able to share, nor even perhaps to comprehend, the experience of the addicts, who form the overwhelming majority of science fiction readers, and to whom, naturally, entertainment is not incidental but essential.' For many readers and viewers, the shock of dysrecognition and their addiction to sf assume cosmic importance, and their identification with the genre takes on a religious fervour. Discovering sf can open a portal into a better, brighter world; the world of the imagination.

Familiar sf ingredients include: utopian or dystopian societies, the end of the world, post-apocalypse, time travel, robots/artificial intelligence, virtual reality/cyberspace, the misappliance of science, technological advances, space exploration, first contact (home or away), alien invasion, space opera, evolution/mutation, genetics, the human mindscape. Of course, it's what the filmmakers do with these ingredients that matters. In addition to the satisfaction of a good story well told, the best sf sparks a frisson of potential or flash of insight into ways that these issues could affect our lives today, tomorrow or the day after. It engages the mind as well as the heart, and offers an all-important thrill of possibility, a genuine sense of wonder.

Genre: Science Fiction And Horror

Sf and horror have a long and close association. Films like *Alien* and *The Thing* fuse horror tropes with those of sf to prey on our unconscious fears. Monster movies have been big business since the heyday of Universal Studios in the 1930s, when science offered handy, if illogical, new rationales for monsters which appealed to the horror audience. Science also unleashed the most terrifying weapon of all, the A-Bomb, instilling fears of megadeaths and mutations. Hollywood quickly exploited these fears. Note there are no friendly giant movie dolphins or koalas, only spiders, ants, gorillas, alligators, octopi; creatures that gave us nightmares even before they became several storeys high.

Susan Sontag said that all sf movies are about disaster, but in truth almost all movies involve disaster for someone. We don't want to see characters having a good time, we want to see what happens when things go horribly wrong. You don't believe me? Well, would you pay to see *Airplanes That Land Safely*? In horror and/or sf, things go wrong on a grand scale. Future societies are far more likely to be dystopian than utopian. For every responsible scientist there are a hundred mad or misguided ones. When machines grow self-aware, watch out; they don't address the poverty gap or feed the world or cure cancer, and they're far from content being servants of mankind. They take on our basest characteristics: jealousy, anger, greed, delusions of grandeur, and we become secondhand victims of our own flaws. Corporations are rarely benevolent; instead they are unrestrained, duplicitous and often lethal. Governments will go to any lengths to pull triggers, press red buttons and take out by any means necessary those who interfere with their activities. And woe betide the first genuine alien emissary to visit Earth – movies have shown us time and again the welcome they'll get. In an uncertain world, horror and sf are complementary bedfellows, and their union supplies many vicarious chills.

Genre: Science Fiction And Fantasy

If horror is a cousin of sf, then fantasy is its bastard sibling (often called science fantasy; oxymoronically, as it has nothing to do with science). The genres are conflated because they both impart a sense of wonder, transport us to impossible places and show us things we've never seen. However, I'd like to disconnect them and offer my less than humble opinion that the inbuilt formulaic clichés of fantasy cinema render it the intellectual inferior of science fiction. And before you throw objects, I agree with you – far too many sf movies employ horrendous clichés of their own. Most sf films are pale imitations of sf literature, marketed by the studios to people who wouldn't normally like it in an attempt to generate maximum profits.

Fantasy movies offer undeniable spectacle but little speculation, remaining closer to their literary roots than sf movies. Too often, fantasy relies upon an exhausted adventure formula: the hero(es) sets off on a quest to find an amulet and/or save a kingdom. Their journey is a camping holiday with assorted trolls and goblins along for the ride. En route, the motley crew is chased by things that become progressively uglier, larger and nastier, and they must contend with treachery in their midst before successfully overcoming all obstacles and achieving their goal. When done well, as in the *Lord Of The Rings* trilogy, this can be exciting and look great. But it always feels the same, and I can't suspend my disbelief. The biggest problem with fantasy is its inbuilt get-out-of-jail-free card … magic. Gaping plot-hole? No problem, magic'll stitch it up. Impossible situation? Worry not, magic has just the *deus ex machina* for you. Gandalf's been imprisoned for eternity atop an impossibly tall tower? Never mind, he can just hop on a passing eagle. Watch any fantasy movie and you'll find examples. This easy way out negates speculation and intelligent plotting, and devalues a genre that has much going for it visually.

Science Fiction And 'Sci-fi'

Sf author Frederik Pohl wrote 'When print science fiction is translated into film science fiction the subtle parts are left out.' The media coined a pejorative term for these commercial mutations, which unfortunately has become the default for all science fiction: 'sci-fi'. Harlan Ellison, sf's most strident voice, summarised the distinction: 'The public image of what *is*, and what *ain't*, science fiction film – an image as twisted as one of Tod Browning's freaks – is the result of decades of paralogia, arrogant stupidity, conscious flummery, and amateurism that have comprised the universal curriculum of *milieu* that passes for filmic education for a gullible audience. If it goes bangity-bang in space; if it throbs and screams and breaks out of its shell with slimy malevolence; if it seeks to enslave your body, your mind, your gonads or your planet; if it looks cuddly and beeps a lot, it's "sci-fi". We pronounce that: *skiffy*. And if you love fantasy, you'll *love* skiffy. And skiffy is to science fiction as Attila was to good table manners.'

Skiffy is what happens when you *remove* the science and allow the fantastic free rein. It still oozes over us today, as studios chase extra noughts at the box office by churning out endless sequels and remakes, infantilising their product to attract a younger audience. This usually results in irreparable damage to the quality and credibility of the film (e.g. *Terminator 3*). But this is the way the studios want it; a younger audience equals a larger audience.

In truth, it also stems from the general decline in scientific awareness. Few people care about non-science, so there's no incentive to get it right. *So many* sf films are spoilt by producers figuring that because they don't understand it neither will the guy in the street, and they're mostly right. Unlike stars, sets and FX, science doesn't slap the money on the screen. However, my contention is that the best sf movies generate the greatest sense of wonder by maintaining a disciplined internal logic and confronting difficult issues with intelligence and sensitivity. *Blade Runner* implicitly condemns racism by raising philosoph-ical and theological questions about what it means to be 'human' – if we create Replicants in our image, are they not us? *Invasion Of The Body Snatchers* posits a scenario in which the 'human' becomes alien, and being alien may be preferable to being human. *2001: A Space Odyssey* questions the qualitative difference between a super-advanced alien civilisation and our concept of God. *Gattaca* portrays an all-too plausible society in which genetic profiling allows us to play God and relegate 'ordinary' non-engineered people to second-class citizens. *Avalon* offers a tuned-out reality in which people choose to play a lethal cyberspace game rather than conform in a world that is rotting away. *The Day The Earth Stood Still* suggests that our species' best police force may be a more powerful extra-terrestrial race. Movies like these offer us new perspectives from which to view the world.

The World Of Tomorrow

Fantasy escapes from the real world, but sf originates there. Robert Silverberg said '… I think one role of science fiction is to serve as an insulator against what Alvin Toffler called "Future Shock" … We may reach a point where we're horrified by what's coming next, but at least we can't say we're surprised by it.' Biotech, nanotech, wearable computing, cybernetics, biometrics: these concepts are familiar because sf prepared us for them. Captain Kirk stuck a silly plastic card into his chair to record his Captain's Log; now we insert much smaller cards into our cameras and use portable electronic devices to transmit images instantly to our friends, or access the cyber universe of the Internet. The design of the Enterprise crew's communicators wasn't light years (distance, George, not time) away from mobile phones. The astronauts in *2001* carried portable flat-screen TVs; now laptop and note-book computers are *de rigueur* on Starbucks sofas, where people tap away while listening to a gadget the size of a pack of cigarettes that holds their entire music collection.

Sf asks us to consider the big 'what ifs' of tomorrow, while skiffy needs us to hang our brains on a peg to administer itself with a hypodermic. The debate about the environment may have been globally warmed by *The Day After Tomorrow*, but no-one takes it seriously as prediction; they just munch popcorn as a CGI Statue Of Liberty remains defiantly upright against the world's biggest tidal wave. A few celluloid prophecies will be powerful, thought-provoking, awe-inspiring and visionary. Mostly though, they'll be Hollywood junk. Fans will still run (or hover, or teleport) along to the multiplex; like Jawas in the Tatooine desert living on scraps, they'll forgive scientific inaccuracies, cardboard characters and ludicrous plots as long as they get the spectacle.

You may be thinking I'm pretty down on sf. On the contrary, I love it, which is why I've written this book. But can you imagine how marvellous it would be if commercial considerations were secondary to a sense of wonder achieved through scientific accuracy, plot consistency and character development? For the foreseeable future, however, we'll have to make do. If fewer stupid science fiction films were made, maybe we'd be inspired to become more open-minded, use our imagination more and progress faster. But that's a different book, and would make us a different species.

NB As I said, this is a personal overview, and as such I have made clear my top ten films by capping the titles in their entries.

9: The Future As It Was Yesterday
(1900–1936)

*'I make use of physics. He fabricates. I go to the Moon in a
cannon-ball discharged from a gun. There is no fabrication
here [emphasis added]. He goes to Mars in an airship, which
he constructs of a metal that does away with the law of gravita-
tion. That's all very fine, but show me this metal. Let him
produce it.'*

Jules Verne (author, on H.G. Wells' novel *The First Men
In The Moon*, proving that 'science' fiction has always been
a relative concept)

The Magic Of Cinema: Smoke And Mirrors

Strange but true: 'cinema' first appeared as a construct in an
1886 'science fiction' story, Villiers de L'Isle-Adam's *L'Ève
Future*. In the story, a female dancer is captured in full movement and sound by projecting images photographed onto glass
plates, exemplifying the ability of 'science fiction' to extrapo-
late the future from present technology – and to bring on the
dancing girls. I place the term 'science fiction' in quotes
because it would be another 43 years before it was coined!
Thus the idea of sf cinema existed long before the term itself.

The earliest sf silents were little more than fairground fancies,
utilising prototypical 'special effects' – illusionistic flourishes
with objects appearing, disappearing and flying in stop-motion
or multiple exposure – but audiences were wowed. Especially at
the Theatre Robert-Houdin in Paris. If you thought the maiden
voyage to Earth's satellite was undertaken by Apollo 11 in 1969,
you'd be wrong, and not because it was really a Hollywood

soundstage. Mankind's first giant leap was taken 67 years earlier by cinema's premier fantasist, Georges Méliès.

Le Voyage Dans La Lune
[A Trip To The Moon] (1902, Fr.)

Prod/Dir/Scr: Georges Méliès
St: Méliès, Bleuette Bernon, Victor André

In 1902 the medium of cinema was the newest attraction in town. The Lumière brothers' one-reel social documents and Méliès' blend of trick cinematography and stage showmanship drew curious crowds to their theatres every night. Méliès' 15-minute astral voyage combined the ideas of proto-sf authors: the 'space cannon' firing explorers to their destination was from Jules Verne's 1862 novel *From The Earth To The Moon*, while H.G. Wells' 1901 novel *The First Men In The Moon* provided the alien race of Selenites.

Méliès did not make 'science fiction' films, he was simply the first magician to work with moving pictures. *A Trip To The Moon* is camp cabaret: a troupe of chorus girls loads the voyagers into the 'space cannon', the 'stars' they pass en route are pretty dancers, and their projectile hits the man in the Moon squarely in the eye. The lobster-clawed Selenites disappear in a puff of smoke when struck, and our heroes have no difficulty breathing in a vacuum.

One later film, *An Impossible Voyage* (1904), featured an impressive model train zooming away on a return trip to the Sun. In 1913, following a run of bad luck and waning popularity, Méliès' company went bankrupt. Despite this, and the candyfloss he often produced, his status as the pioneer illusionist of fantastic cinema is assured.

Paris Qui Dort
[aka The Crazy Ray] (1923, Fr.)

Dir/Scr: René Clair; *Prod:* Henri Diamant-Berger
St: Henri Rolland, Madeleine Rodrigue, Albert Préjean

Semi-surrealist dreamlike fantasy in which a mad scientist stops time in Paris. Its inhabitants are frozen in a temporal limbo, with the exception of anyone in the air. Clair's camera roams Paris, now a truly enchanted city, as protagonist Albert ventures forth from his Eiffel Tower base to wander through the unmoving sleepers.

Aelita (1924, USSR)

Dir: Yakov Protazanov; *Scr:* Fyodor Otsep, Aleksei Faiko, based on the novel by Aleksei Tolstoy
St: Yulia Solntseva, Igor Ilyinsky, Nikolai Tsereteli

Aelita, Queen Of Mars, observes young Russian engineer Los through a fantastic lens, and he in turn dreams of her. He pilots his own space ship to the Red planet, where he introduces Aelita to kissing (so how … oh, never mind), and the repressive Martian monarchy to communism. Los liberates the proletarian slaves (predating *Metropolis*) and inspires a revolution to overthrow the regime, establishing The People's Republic Of Mars! The design of this frothy but fun Bolshevik propagandist fantasy mixes cubist, constructivist and expressionist motifs to good effect.

The City Is Human

Technological advances of the Modernist era, including those of cinema, proved inspirational to artists and filmmakers who explored the new possibilities around them. Increasing urbanisation inevitably led to speculation about technological and social trends. At the root of all sf is the question 'What if?' The first major question to emerge in sf cinema was: What if cities just keep on growing?

Metropolis (1926, Ger.) ★★★★★

Dir: Fritz Lang; *Prod:* Erich Pommer; *Scr:* Lang and Thea von Harbou
St: Alfred Abel, Gustav Fröhlich, Brigitte Helm, Rudolf Klein-Rogge

Biplanes buzz around impossibly tall skyscrapers and traffic clogs aerial freeways. The megacity of tomorrow is a paradise for the ruling elite, but hell for the enslaved drones whose toil at the underground generators provides the city's power. Freder, foppish son of city master Joh Fredersen, falls for Maria, a kindergarten teacher and covert preacher of human rights to the drones. Upon following her to the subterranean levels, he is horrified to discover their plight. Fredersen, fearing Maria's influence, has mad scientist Rotwang kidnap her and create an evil robot duplicate to undo her good work. The android's risqué turn in the Yoshiwara brothel (more dancing girls!) inflames the workers' passions. However, Fredersen's plan backfires when they revolt against the machines, causing a flood that nearly destroys them all. Freder helps Maria to escape from Rotwang and they rescue the workers' children. The near-disaster causes the slaves and masters to vow to work together in future.

After studying architecture, graphic art and design, Fritz Lang was wounded in the First World War. He collaborated on the scenario of Robert Wiene's *Das Kabinett des Dr. Caligari* [*The Cabinet Of Dr. Caligari*] (1919). Made by the giant Ufa studio, it introduced the highly stylized look of the Expressionist art movement into cinema: distorted, angular sets, foreshortened perspectives and psychologically unsettling proximities. Lang carried this aesthetic into his own films. The spectacular New York skyline inspired his great dystopian vision, which he co-wrote with his wife. It was released in 1926, a landmark year that also saw Hugo Gernsback coin the term 'scientifiction' for his new pulp magazine *Amazing Stories*.

Metropolis has exerted a powerful influence over sf films as diverse as *Blade Runner* and *Dr. Strangelove*, and is one of the medium's greatest achievements. The story is overly melodramatic (the workers' revolt stretches credibility to breaking point), but the concept and design of the great Gothic city is awesome, imparting the giddying sense of wonder that only the best sf can attain. The film's issues of labour relations, although oversimplified, are still relevant today. Thirty thousand extras toiled in conditions not unlike the workers' to realise Lang's vision, cementing his reputation as a tyrant and nearly bankrupting Ufa. Scenes of exhausted workers struggling to keep dials moving on gigantic machines, shuffling shaven-headed masses queueing for elevators at shift change, and the Frankensteinian transformation of the robot Maria are among the chief iconography of sf cinema.

In 1984, Italian musician/producer Giorgio Moroder released a colourised and re-edited version with an electronic/rock music score that is better than its critical reception suggests.

Lang only directed one other sf film, the rarely screened *Woman In The Moon* [*Frau Im Mond*] (1929). Its astronauts, like Méliès', are able to breathe and walk normally on the Moon, but its rocket science was advanced, and it introduced the pre-launch countdown later adopted by NASA for its space programme. Films like *M* and *Die Testament Der Dr. Mabuse* enhanced Lang's reputation, but he fled Germany in 1933 when Hitler, who adored *Metropolis*, sought to appoint him chief filmmaker of the Third Reich. Lang enjoyed an illustrious career in America, where he died in 1976.

Things To Come (1936, UK) ★★★

Dir: William Cameron Menzies; *Prod:* Alexander Korda; *Scr:* H.G. Wells and Lajos Biro
St: Raymond Massey, Ralph Richardson, Cedric Hardwicke

Everytown, 1940: Before the Cabal and Passworthy families can celebrate Christmas, World War II breaks out. Humanity is decimated, and survivors are gripped by a grim 'wandering plague'. By 1970 the war has run its course, and isolated tribes fight for control of oil. An aircraft lands in the ruins of Everytown, piloted by John Cabal. After being captured by the local Boss, Cabal is rescued by fellow Men In Black, airmen from 'Wings Over The World', a global quasi-governmental organisation. By 2036, the airmen have reconstructed Everytown as a domed utopia, and a 'space gun' is built to shoot mankind to the Moon. An anti-technology riot led by sculptor Theotocopoulos fails to prevent the launch of the capsule containing the youngest descendents of the Cabals and Passworthys. In a giant observatory, their fathers track their progress and reflect on mankind's destiny.

Desperate to be taken seriously as an authority who could solve the world's problems if leaders would only see things his way, Wells often suffered rejection and ignominy. Movies of his 'scientific romance' novels like *The Invisible Man* (1933) were not to his liking either. When Alexander Korda raised nearly $1.5 million to film the 'future history' *The Shape Of Things To Come*, Wells seized the opportunity to deliver his grandest polemic, in all its majestic glory and infuriating pomposity. His socialist ideology is questionable – progress equals scientific 'reason' wielded by incorruptible dictators who wear slippers and speak BBC English – and the narrative style is stale and didactic. Characters are vehicles for ideas. Art and science are opposing principles, and the artists' naive attempt to challenge space travel is easily thwarted. The 'space gun' borrowed from Verne is as preposterous as in *A Trip To The Moon*.

And yet *Things To Come* has many virtues, not least its design. Menzies, a former illustrator and production designer on *Gone With The Wind*, storyboarded every scene. Wells hated the Gothic splendour of Lang's 'silly' *Metropolis*; consequently, sections of his future city look like precursors of a modern antiseptic megamall. Overall though, 2036 Everytown is spectacular, based on designs by architects including Walter Gropius and Le Corbusier.

Wells' prediction of the start of WWII was uncannily close. His emphasis on controlling oil production, situating the airmen's base in Basra, is particularly prescient in the light of the US-led invasion of Iraq which many regard as a strategy to do exactly that. The effects of the ravages of plague are chilling, and Cabal's final question as he watches his daughter's capsule recede, 'All the Universe, or nothingness – which shall it be?' still raises hairs on the back of one's neck.

Nevertheless, the film bombed, skittling the chances of other expensive sf movies getting off the ground. When the real WWII began three years later, the world didn't want more future speculations or dystopias. In fact, it didn't want sf films, period. The next important entry in the genre would not arrive for nearly fifteen years.

8: Fear Is The Key (1950–1959)

'People, by the 50s, had lost their optimistic confidence in the ability of science to fulfil all the dreams of mankind; instead, you saw science about to fulfil all the nightmares of mankind. The prospect of nuclear war ... was hours away.'

J.G. Ballard (author)

Science Fiction's Second Golden Age

The Golden Age of American pulp sf magazines began during the Depression of the 1930s and made it through the 1940s, prompting a surge in sf novel publication. The sf film boom didn't arrive until the following decade due to the slight distraction of WWII. British and American studios produced war propaganda or home-and-hearth melodramas to boost morale; sf output was confined to children's adventure serials like *Flash Gordon* (1936–40) and *Buck Rogers* (1939), which were fantasies that utilised sf trimmings and influenced the *Star Wars* saga. *Astounding* had led the magazine field for years, and new additions *Galaxy* and *The Magazine Of Fantasy And Science Fiction* made a big splash. Even prestigious mainstream mags like the *Saturday Evening Post* embraced sf. Naturally, Hollywood sought to cash in on its popularity.

Are They Really Out There –
Or Are They Already Here?

In many ways, post-WWII history equals American history. In 1950, with the enemy vanquished and the economy flourishing, the world's first Hyperpower looked to the future with optimism, excepting the unquantified threat from behind the

Iron Curtain, the futile Korean War and the fallout from becoming the first nation to nuke another. (In a famous example of sf prediction, author Cleve Cartmill's short story about an atomic bomb, *Deadline*, in the March 1944 edition of *Astounding*, attracted the attention of Manhattan Project scientists and Federal security agencies. They investigated Cartmill and editor John W. Campbell on suspicion of leaking military secrets, but were eventually convinced that the story was written using publicly available scientific data. This was over a year before Robert Oppenheimer's first successful A-bomb test at Alamogordo, New Mexico!)

At Nagasaki and Hiroshima, science fiction became unthinkable fact. The US government deflected fears by convincing its people that over in the USSR old Joe Stalin was far worse, and his evil doctrine could spread like a virus. America became increasingly paranoid about 'Reds in the bed'. The administration was hostile to the influx of Eastern European nationals, particularly in Hollywood, which had long been regarded as a hotbed of subversion. Senator Joseph McCarthy's notorious House Committee on Un-American Activities (HUAC) was set up to unearth communist infiltration, either real or imagined. Colleagues were forced to testify against each other or face prison. Fritz Lang was among the blacklisted, barred from making films. The deep irony was that these 'witch hunts' smacked more of the communism that the Committee was ostensibly there to weed out. Hollywood's response was a series of coded messages protesting the erosion of freedom and democracy. To openly criticise the government risked denunciation or jail, so filmmakers borrowed another threat as a metaphor for its abuses. That threat came, of course, from the stars. Following media speculation about the capture of an alien spaceship in Roswell, New Mexico, in 1947, UFO sightings became the latest urban myth. Beleaguered citizens had yet another reason to be spooked, and to keep watching the skies.

Your Place ...
Destination Moon (1950, USA) ★★

Dir: Irving Pichel; *Prod:* George Pal; *Scr:* (Alford) 'Rip' Van Ronkel, Robert A. Heinlein, James O'Hanlon
St: John Archer, Warner Anderson, Dick Wesson

This documentary/realist tale of the first manned space flight was loosely based on Heinlein's juvenile novel *Rocketship Galileo*. It has dated badly despite impressive backdrops by the celebrated astronomical artist Chesley Bonestell, and Oscar-winning special effects. The writing and direction are lumpen, and the plot is propaganda. Heinlein's axes grind loudly: the unity of scientific and military methods (he also wrote *Starship Troopers*); preservation of capitalism against the communist threat; and ineffectual government. The expedition is corporately funded, takes off in defiance of official orders, and the Moon is a vital (but totally illogical) vantage point from which to launch nuclear strikes against the Russians. Scientist Cargraves shows none of Neil Armstrong's humility when claiming the Moon: 'By the grace of God and in the name of the United States of America.'

The first sf movie event of the 50s sent a defiant message in support of the American pioneering spirit and provided a 'hard science' sense of wonder to wow the post-war boom audience. And it did, returning over $3.5million at the box office against a cost of $500,000. It launched the career of producer Pal (another East European émigré), beginning his long and fruitful association with the genre. *DM* blazed the trail for many schlock space missions to follow, including *Rocketship X-M* (1950) and *Flight To Mars* (1951), and alerted the studios to the commercial potential of science fiction films.

On the predictive level there are similarities in look and procedure between *DM* and the 1969 Apollo 11 Moon landing. A Woody Woodpecker cartoon explains the principles of rocket science to the group of industrialists (and to the audience). There's also a thriller element: the rocket has too little fuel to return from the Moon with its full payload, but after jettisoning all non-essential objects it is still too heavy, by approximately the weight of one man. Eventually the radio equipment is sacrificed. Imperialist ideology aside, I wish I could have gauged *DM* in its own time. For all its flaws, it took the genre in the opposite direction to monster movies and space opera serials. It was a welcome, if plodding, leap for mankind.

When Worlds Collide (1951, USA) ★★½

Dir: Rudolph Maté; *Prod:* George Pal; *Scr:* Sidney Boehm
St: Richard Derr, Barbara Rush, John Hoyt

Pal followed *DM* with an adaptation of Philip Wylie and Edwin Balmer's tale of a race to build a spaceship to escape Armageddon. Earth is about to be destroyed by a wandering dying star, Bellus, and 40 people will continue mankind by populating Bellus' lone planet, Zyra. Like *DM*, the project is funded by private enterprise and, echoing *Things To Come* and *Metropolis*, the citizens revolt against technology (this time with the more logical motivation that everyone left behind will perish). Plausibility is secondary to adventure and melodrama, but the launch of the new Ark as it is attacked by desperate hordes and the cataclysmic destruction of the Earth are impressive FX sequences.

The launch of the rocketship on rails from a steep ramp was echoed in Gerry Anderson's 1960s' juvenile TV show, *Fireball XL5*. The Empire State Building protruding above the waves after a tidal wave destroys New York anticipates the city's fate in *A.I.* (2002) and *The Day After Tomorrow* (2004). Maté photographed Carl Dreyer's horror classic *Vampyr* (1931), and Boehm scripted Fritz Lang's searing post-blacklist noir, *The Big Heat* (1953).

This Island Earth (1955, USA) ★★★½

Dir: Joseph Newman; *Prod:* William Alland; *Scr:* Franklin Coen, Edward O'Callaghan, from the novel by Raymond F. Jones
St: Rex Reason, Jeff Morrow, Faith Domergue

When jet-setting physicist Cal Meacham loses control of his plane, an unearthly green glow lands it safely. Next he receives a bunch of strange parts and a phonebook size schematic from which he builds an 'Interociter' – a weird triangular TV set. From its screen a high-domed, white-haired man called Exeter invites him to join a scientific think-tank. Meacham is flown by remote-controlled plane to meet eminent international scientists, including Dr Ruth Adams. Despite having once been, er, friendly, she denies knowing him. Exeter and looka-like Brack have assembled an elite group of nuclear researchers. Not before time, Cal smells a rat. He learns their hosts are aliens who need uranium to shore up their planet's defensive shield against their mortal enemies. The aliens destroy the mansion, and Cal and Ruth's plane is swallowed up by the alien ship. After acclimatising to space travel in pressurisation tubes they are taken to Metaluna, arriving just in time to witness the planet's destruction as Zahgon ships guide flaming meteors through the spent protective shield. Metalunan leader The Monitor orders Cal and Ruth's execution, but a meteor strikes the complex. With Exeter's help they take off, accompanied by a slave-mutant stowaway that mortally wounds Exeter before being smeared over the floor by the pressure. Back on Earth, Exeter releases their plane and pilots his ship to a watery grave.

You're probably thinking this sounds like pure skiffy. And you're right. Exeter and Brack might as well have 'We're aliens!' tattooed on their enormous foreheads but Cal takes an age to twig; Fox Mulder would have got it instantly. Why do advanced aliens need Earth scientists? Especially ones as dumb as these; Ruth calls the resident cat Neutron 'because he's so positive'. God help the Metalunans if Earth's best don't know that *neut*rons possess neither positive nor negative charge. It makes no sense that Ruth denies knowing Cal. He displays no symptoms of brainwashing, unlike the obviously zombified scientists. The stupidly named Monitor says his race will colonise Earth, but they're in no hurry considering their planet is being bombed into a sun.

Skiffy apart though, *TIE* is a film that gets under your skin, and it is the Metalunan section that fans love best. Universal brought in Jack Arnold to reshoot Newman's efforts. Peter Nicholls contends that the colourful Metalunan sequences 'contain some of the best SF imagery in cinema, as meteors rain down upon the planet's pitted, ruined surface and the sky is ablaze with the light of warfare. As vivid adventure – admittedly at a juvenile level – *This Island Earth* remains even today one of the better SF movies.' I nearly imploded with joy and awe when I saw it on TV as a kid, and it's this evocation of wonder that makes critics forgive its boneheadedness.

In the spoof TV series *Mystery Science Theater 3000* (1990–93), an astronaut and two robot companions are held captive on an orbiting ship by a mad scientist. For no good reason they're forced to watch bad films which they wisecrack through. In the movie *MST3K* (1996) they trash *This Island Earth*; a must-see for fans. I love the comment when Cal and Ruth's fingers lock around the handles of the pressurisation tubes, and Exeter explains that they're magnetised: 'And if your hands were made of metal, that would mean something.' Best of all though is a quip over the opening credits: 'Let's see here … Shatner … Shatner … nope, doesn't look like he's in this one, we're safe.'

FORBIDDEN PLANET (1956, USA) *****

Dir: Fred McLeod Wilcox; *Prod:* Nicholas Nayfack; *Scr:* Cyril Hume, from a story by Irving Block and Allen Adler
St: Walter Pidgeon, Anne Francis, Leslie Nielsen, Warren Stevens

United Planets space cruiser C57-D lands on Altair 4 to discover the fate of the ship *Bellerophon*. The crew are greeted by a sophisticated robot called Robby who transports them to Morbius, the last surviving crew member of the *Bellerophon*. Morbius resents their presence, but gives them a tour of the impressive home he has built from the wreckage. To his chagrin, the men are more impressed by his teenage daughter Altaira, and she by them. Morbius warns Commander Adams that he and his men must leave, describing a malevolent invisible force that killed the other survivors, including his wife. The men return to their ship full of questions: what was this force and why did it not kill Morbius? How could he have built the house or Robby when his expertise was in languages? Who'll get lucky with Altaira?

When the invisible force targets the ship and crew, Morbius reluctantly leads them beneath the house to reveal a breathtaking sight: endless banks of vast subterranean machines built by the planet's long dead race, the Krell. The machines have boosted Morbius' intelligence to superhuman levels, but in doing so unleashed the amplified force of his primal subconscious rage; the same force that wiped out the Krell. When Adams insists on taking Altaira back to Earth, the house comes under attack. Impregnable alloy shutters are ripped asunder and the power dials on the Krell machines overload as Morbius' jealous id seeks revenge. Morbius' final act of sacrifice blows his mind, leaving Altaira in Adams' arms.

Effects artist Block moved Shakespeare's *The Tempest* from Bermuda to Altair 4: Prospero = Morbius; Miranda = Altaira; and Ariel = Robby. Caliban is ingeniously reinvented as the monster from the id. *FP* introduced a new maturity to sf cinema, daring to suggest that evil is located in the human subconscious, and that Morbius' fury is triggered by protective feelings or even sexual desire for Altaira.

Most of the personnel had never done sf; director Wilcox was best known for *Lassie Come Home*! Aging star Pidgeon got to dress in black and wear a goatee, while bland Nielsen went on to achieve fame against type in the spoof comedies *Police Squad* and *Naked Gun*. The United Planets inspired Gene Roddenberry's philanthropic Federation of races in *Star Trek*. (Adams' privilege of rank in getting the girl also paved the way for the conquests of one James Tiberius Kirk.) Despite the omens, the curious enterprise (sorry) worked like a technicolour cinemascope dream. Frederik Pohl recalled colleague Lester Del Rey's remark upon leaving the cinema: 'That's the first original science fiction film I've seen that could have made a fine novelette for *Astounding*.'

My first viewing of *FP*, in the early teen years so perfect for discovering sf, was pure enlightenment. It inspired in me the same tingling awe as certain sf literature had already. The gorgeous production design; the screeching, bleeping electronic tonalities of Louis and Bebe Barron; the coolest movie robot ever; the multifarious charms of Anne Francis … it draws you in like only the best sf can. The id-monster, animated by Disney's Josh Meador, is like an adult Tasmanian Devil, and it scared the bejesus out of me. Robby, with his visible moving parts, jolly personality and inability to harm humans (adopting Isaac Asimov's Three Laws of Robotics), became a legendary sf icon.

However, the curse of genuine sf struck. Although now regarded as a classic, *FP* was too sophisticated to attract a wide audience and only recouped half of its $1.6 million budget while schlock like *Earth Vs. The Flying Saucers* made a fortune for a fraction of the outlay. Ain't no justice.

… Or Mine?

The pioneering spirit of going boldly (to unsplit the infinitive) where no man etc., exploring other planets and meeting alien races was all very well, but for the studios it was a helluva lot cheaper to bring those critters here.

The Thing [aka The Thing From Another World] (1951, USA) ★★★½

Dir: Christian Nyby, Howard Hawks (uncredited); *Prod:* Hawks; *Scr:* Charles Lederer, based on the story *Who Goes There?* by Don A. Stuart
St: Kenneth Tobey, Margaret Sheridan, Robert Cornthwaite, James Arness

The personnel of an Arctic military/scientific research base investigate a strange craft buried in a nearby glacier. On closer inspection they find that it is a gigantic flying saucer. Captain Hendry orders the use of thermite to melt the ice around it but the explosive also destroys the ship. The body of a pilot is discovered nearby and is brought back encased in ice. However, the creature thaws out and after a battle with the dogs it escapes, minus an arm. Tests on the appendage reveal the creature is a vegetable-based life form that requires blood to survive. Scientist Carrington 'plants' the arm in greenhouse soil to see if it will grow. The Thing, limb now regrown, has its own uses for the greenhouse, planting seeds there to grow a few comrades. It stalks the base, and the scientists and military must work together to destroy it. Hendry kills the growing lifeforms and his men manage to repel the Thing. They set an electrical trap for it, into which it falls and is fried.

High praise has been lavished on *TTFAW*, but this puzzles me; it's good, no doubt, but surely not a *classic*. It departs from the story, written pseudonymously by *Astounding* editor John W. Campbell, in one crucial respect: in the film the alien can't adopt human form. Hawks sacrificed its place as the first in the bodysnatcher cycle (i.e., commies, sorry, aliens take over ordinary people and no one can trust their neighbours any more), merely warming us up for a superior alien vegetable in *Invasion Of The Body Snatchers*. This is probably heresy, but I prefer John Carpenter's 1982 remake.

'It is important that we don't confuse the Frankenstein type of film with the science fiction picture,' wrote Hawks. 'The first film is an out-and-out horror thriller based on that which is impossible. The science fiction film is based on that which is unknown, but which is given credibility by the use of scientific facts ...' By using a crummy vegenstein monster Hawks invalidates his claim; *The Thing* has no more scientific credibility than *Spider Man*. One character exclaims: 'An intellectual carrot — the mind boggles' and he ain't kidding. Its big bald head, ridged monobrow, claw-gloves and Michael Myers-style black overalls, are pure B-movie. Wisely, it is seldom seen, and when it is, it's a 'jump' moment. Tension is reinforced by claustrophobic sets and the constant 'where is it?' threat. Paranoia is high, with subtexts regarding the 'coldness' of Russia, and the futility of science against the military method. By trying to reason with the alien Carrington is viewed with suspicion; a commie within. Anticipating *IOTBS* and *Alien*, he expresses admiration for the creature's lack of empathy or conscience. In a nice touch, the message to keep the Thing alive comes through only after it is dead. Lone female Nikki is feisty but infatuated with Hendry and, although she comes up with the method of killing the Thing, it is in a gender-patronising way: she suggests they cook it like any other vegetable.

Hawks is widely acknowledged as co-director, chaperoning his ex-editor Nyby and incorporating his own trademark style. *The Thing* is an effective shocker but missed an opportunity to criticise the HUAC 'inquisition' that pitted Americans against their fellows. Or, Hawks may have wanted to emphasise the threat to the American Way – the film's final warning is, after all, 'Keep watching the skies!'

THE DAY THE EARTH STOOD STILL
(1951, USA) *****

Dir: Robert Wise; *Prod:* Julian Blaustein; *Scr:* Edmund H. North, from the story *Farewell To The Master* by Harry Bates
St: Michael Rennie, Patricia Neal, Hugh Marlowe, Sam Jaffe

An alien spacecraft lands in Washington DC. A helmeted humanoid figure exits, accompanied by a giant robot. First contact hits an immediate snag as the alien is winged by a bullet from a trigger-happy soldier. The robot's visor slowly opens and the glint in its eye vaporises tanks. The alien barks a command and its visor closes. After being taken to hospital the alien, Klaatu, absconds and a full-scale alien-hunt is mobilised. Under the alias of 'Carpenter' he rents a room from widow Helen Benson and befriends her lonely son Bobby. One night Bobby follows Carpenter to the landing site, and watches as the immobile robot stirs and fells the guards, allowing Carpenter to enter the ship. Later, Bobby tells his mother and her shallow boyfriend Tom.

After enlisting the help of Prof. Barnhardt, Klaatu prepares to meet representatives of Earth's nations – scientists and thinkers, *not* politicians – by staging a demonstration of technological superiority, causing the Earth to literally stand still for 30 minutes as all electrical activity is neutralised. During the shutdown he explains his identity and his mission to Helen. Meanwhile, Tom has alerted the authorities. Klaatu gives Helen a message for the robot, Gort, should anything happen to him. They approach the ship in a taxi but are intercepted by the Army, and Klaatu is shot, seemingly fatally. Helen's message stops Gort unleashing his terrible revenge. He takes her into the ship and goes to recover Klaatu's body. As the military disperses the group of international scientists, Klaatu emerges with a sobering message for the world: technological advancement will spread humans' natural belligerence to the stars and pose a threat to the harmony of life across the Universe. This cannot be allowed to happen: 'Your choice is simple. Join us and live in peace or pursue your present course and face obliteration.' He leaves the nations of Earth to decide their fate.

The Day The Earth Stood Still is a bona-fide masterpiece, imparting the most sublime sense of wonder. As in *Forbidden Planet*, there is a conflict between science, religion and politics: good and evil are not external Manichean forces but internal human choices, and being the good guys is subjective. Wise, editor of *Citizen Kane*, whose first sf film this was, told Frederik Pohl: 'Here on Earth we must have the greatest egos imaginable to think that we are the only intelligent beings anywhere in this tremendous Universe. And it was very obvious that the film was making a political comment.' It is as critical of American imperialism as *Dr. Strangelove*: when the US Presidential representative assumes the moral high ground, he is silenced by Klaatu. Aggressive small-minded nationalism is the reason he's come.

The film provokes an amazing range of emotions. When Klaatu is shot, it sends a chill of truth down the spine. Gort may be a giant in a rubber suit (7ft 6in Lock Martin, a doorman at Grauman's Chinese Theater on Hollywood Boulevard), but when it loomed over Patricia Neal ready to destroy the Earth, to me it was a real robot with a real doomsday ray in its eye, and I was as terrified as she. Her halting message 'Gort, Klaatu barada nikto!' is sf's most famous alien phrase. The spaceship with its seamless opening is beautiful and *Citizen Kane* composer Bernard Herrmann's score has never been bettered for otherworldly atmosphere. Rennie and Neal are excellent, underplaying to maintain the realistic tone, and Jaffe works well as a wild-haired Einstein clone.

Bates, editor of *Astounding* before John Campbell, was paid a miserly $500 for the rights to his story; the budget for the film was nearly $1million. North discarded Bates' final revelation that the 'Master' of the title was not the alien but the robot. He also pointed up symbolic parallels with Christ: Klaatu, an agent for human change, comes down to Earth, takes the name *Carpenter*, is betrayed, dies and is resurrected before ascending once more. The Hays Censorship office was outraged, insisting this was God's province alone, so Klaatu is only resuscitated for a short time – a compromise the producers hated, but I love. It's important to realise that our tendency to destroy what we don't understand has notched its first galactic casualty, thereby proving Klaatu's point. Many liberal commentators attacked his ultimatum as hypocritical and not exactly advanced, but it is logical in its implication that all humanoid species are inherently warlike and the robots are the only foolproof method of enforcing peace. The confederacy of races has signed up to this, and so must Earth, or pay the ultimate penalty.

Wise deploys codes of documentary-style realism and noir, but Bill Warren's point that it's more like adult films of the period than contemporary sf films tacitly acknowledges that sf films must surmount the stigma. A good sf film is rarely thought of as a good film. *The Day The Earth Stood Still* is a great film, period.

The War Of The Worlds (1953, USA) ★★★½

Dir: Byron Haskin; *Prod:* George Pal; *Scr:* Barré Lyndon, from the novel by H.G. Wells
St: Gene Barry, Anne Robinson, Les Tremayne, Robert Cornthwaite

In 1938, Orson Welles' notorious radio adaptation scandalised the US. His documentary-style drama caused widespread panic as many listeners took first-hand reports of alien invasion for real. Lyndon took Welles' cue and relocated the invasion from Victorian Britain to contemporary California. Martian cylinders land and from them emerge manta-ray-shaped flying craft with cobra-like antennae that spit energy bolts. They cannot be stopped, not even by atomic bombs. Then, when their firepower has crushed the Earth's forces and reduced cities to rubble, they suddenly begin to drop out of the sky. The Martians are fatally susceptible to bacteria, '…the littlest things that God in his wisdom created for the Earth.'

You can only get away with a *deus ex machina* ending (one that comes completely out of nowhere) like this once, but this is the once. The downsides are some poor effects (the ships' strings, ropey Martian ray opticals), uneven acting and syrupy religious piety. But there are many upsides: pacing; Al Nozaki's production and ship design; the model work and blasted street sets; and the cyclopean Martian creature (glimpsed only once, touching Robinson's shoulder). The message to keep watching the skies was reinforced, as was the veiled threat of Russian (or Chinese) supremacy in the arms race. The film was released to selected theatres in the new magnetic stereo sound process and was another critical and commercial triumph for Pal. Gordon Jennings won his third effects Oscar, but sadly didn't live to collect it.

It Came From Outer Space (1953, USA) ★★★½

Dir: Jack Arnold; *Prod:* William Alland; *Scr:* Harry Essex, Ray Bradbury, from a treatment by Bradbury
St: Richard Carlson, Barbara Rush, Charles Drake

John Putnam is an outsider; an astronomer in a desert town with a jealousy-inducing young fiancée and a bunch of kooky theories. When a meteorite lands near his home he investigates the crater and sees a spaceship, but it is buried under a landslide. Of course, no-one believes him, least of all the young Sheriff who covets his girl. When the townspeople start changing (aw, not *again*), he finds the aliens just need the manpower to repair their ship and go home.

One of the best bodysnatcher movies, *ICFOS* survives several looooooming foreground objects (it was made in 3-D) to offer genuine wonder, unsettling mood and some stand-out moments. It is imaginatively directed by Arnold from source material by Bradbury, sf's most poetic/lyrical voice. The alien, a soft-focus jellyfish-thing with a huge eye, and its subjective point of view through a shimmering haze are scary (well, they scared me when I was 11). The desert locations add to the atmosphere, and subjective aerial shots above the roadside telegraph wires are among the most affecting images from my childhood, complemented by really creepy music. The following year, Arnold, Alland, Essex and Carlson reunited for another 3-D film, my favourite monster movie, *Creature From The Black Lagoon*.

Invaders From Mars (1953, USA) ★½

Dir: William Cameron Menzies; *Prod:* Edward L. Alperson, Sr; *Scr:* Richard Blake
St: Jimmy Hunt, Leif Erickson, Helena Carter

Little Jimmy sees a UFO land behind his house, and soon his parents change into Emotionless Fifties Aliens™. Jimmy teams up with a doctor and an astronomer to tackle the rather small Martian green man, and the military blows up the ship. Original writer John Tucker Battle was so angry with the tacked-on 'it was all a dream' ending in the US that he withdrew his name. To be honest, he should have considered doing so anyway, or better still, not have written it in the first place.

The Quatermass Xperiment [aka The Creeping Unknown] (1955, UK) ★★★

Dir: Val Guest; *Prod:* Anthony Hinds; *Scr:* Guest, Richard Landau, based on the BBC TV series by Nigel Kneale
St: Brian Donlevy, Jack Warner, Margia Dean, Richard Wordsworth

Before kids watched the BBC's Doctor Who through their fingers, adults did the same for Kneale's Quatermass serials. The first of three big-screen outings concerns a three-man space mission that returns with only one survivor, Victor Carroon. He is already transforming into an alien fungus that feeds off organic matter. The race is on to stop him, and finally Prof. Quatermass electrocutes him/it in Westminster Abbey. It was made by the UK's Hammer studio, which established an international reputation with superior horror films like *The Mummy* and *Curse Of The Werewolf*. Wordsworth is terrific, eliciting maximum sympathy for the tragic Victor. Donlevy, however, plays Bernard Quatermass as a loudmouthed boor with few endearing qualities.

The sequel, *Quatermass II* (1957) ★★½, builds tension as the Prof. tries to destroy an alien base, made more difficult by the fact that they've taken over the government (see, I *knew* there was an explanation!). One of the best moments is when actor Bryan Forbes is taken over. He later directed *The Stepford Wives* (1975), a stupid, misogynistic trifle about a town where the menfolk replace their wives with sexy, compliant robots. (For reasons best known to his bank manager, Frank Oz directed a more PC remake in 2004.) Val Guest directed *The Day The Earth Caught Fire* (1961), an interesting, very British middle-class tale about the Earth being propelled into the Sun by nuclear tests.

The third film, *Quatermass And The Pit* [aka *Five Million Years To Earth*] (1967) ★★★★, may be the best British sf movie. A London underground tunnel dig unearths very old ape bones and a strange craft. Quatermass finds insectoid remains which he deduces are Martian. He realises that humans are descended from apes altered by the Martians. Power cables revive the ship and it spreads a mental energy across London, causing those with Martian genes to attack those without (kind of similar to but way ahead of *Lifeforce*). It was directed by Roy Ward Baker (Rudolph Cartier did the TV version) and starred Andrew Keir (after André Morell) as the Prof., a better turn than Donlevy's.

Quatermass came to an end in 1980 on TV with *The Quatermass Conclusion*. John Mills played the Prof. Although poorly received, I think it's a fitting finale for a great British institution.

Earth Vs. The Flying Saucers (1956, USA) ★½

Dir: Fred F. Sears; *Prod:* Charles H. Schneer; *Scr:* George Worthing Yates, Raymond T. Marcus
St: Hugh Marlowe, Joan Taylor, Harry Lauter

Not cooped up with the turkeys, mainly due to stop-motion king Ray Harryhausen's spectacular effects. He seamlessly combined his gorgeous flying saucers with stock footage, giving a realism rare in 50s sf films. The aliens, an ancient race from a dying world, receive a traditional military welcome. They give Marlowe's Professor an ultimatum of 60 days for mankind to surrender, because they want to take over peacefully! Why not just zap us like the Martians? Why 60 days? Perhaps it was to ensure that in true James Bond fashion we could develop the means to defeat them – jolly good sports! Despite the destruction of Congress and the Washington monument, the Prof comes up with the goods using magnetism, and so humanity abides once more.

Raymond T. Marcus was a pseudonym of Bernard Gordon, blacklisted by McCarthy. Tim Burton's *Mars Attacks!* (1996) is a wickedly affectionate parody, and the same year's *Independence Day* is a dumb Hollywood update.

INVASION OF THE BODY SNATCHERS
(1956, USA) ★★★★★

Dir: Don Siegel; *Prod:* Walter Wanger; *Scr:* Daniel Mainwaring, from the novel *The Body Snatchers* by Jack Finney
St: Kevin McCarthy, Dana Wynter, Carolyn Jones

In an LA hospital Dr Miles Bennell babbles a crazy story to a psychiatrist, beginning when several people in the town of Santa Mira claim that their nearest and dearest are cold, impersonal imposters. Before long, Miles' friends Jack and Teddy find a body. When he and girlfriend Becky check it out, they see an unfinished duplicate of Jack lying on the pool table. Later at Becky's house, Miles finds an unfinished duplicate of her in the basement. They flee.

Psychiatrist Dan insists they must have imagined the events, but that night in Miles' greenhouse they discover four pods, growing simulacra of them. After 'killing' the pods, they phone for help but the operator is also a pod. Leaving in a car, they find the police are pods too, so they take refuge in Miles' surgery. The townsfolk load giant pods onto trucks, bound for all parts. Jack and Teddy have slept and been taken over, as has Dan. They tell Miles that being a pod is better than being human – no messy emotions like pain or love – but he and Becky flee Santa Mira with the townspeople in hot pursuit. Miles leaves Becky in a mountain cave, where she too succumbs to sleep. When he returns and kisses her he realises she too is a pod. He runs to the highway, where he is picked up and taken to the hospital. The psychiatrist there dismisses Miles' story, but a truck driver is admitted after an accident involving a truck full of large vegetable pods. The psychiatrist calls the FBI.

Don Siegel said 'People are pods ... They have no feelings.

They exist, breathe, sleep. To be a pod means that you have no passion, no anger, the spark has left you ... These pods, who get rid of pain, ill health and mental disturbance are, in a sense, doing good. It happens to leave you with a very dull world, but that ... is the world that most of us live in.' *IOTBS* is the best alien invasion film, a metaphor for the paranoia being fed to the people, and a rallying cry to revoke apathy and embrace our culture before we lose it. Individuality is a Siegel trademark; in *Dirty Harry* (1971), a maverick cop ignores his superiors and adopts criminal methods. Siegel's comments implicitly criticise studio interference that cut much of the humour from *IOTBS*, changed the title (Siegel wanted to call it *Sleep No More* after Hamlet's soliloquy) and imposed the framing device of Miles' story to lighten the ending. Originally, Miles encountered a pod truck on the highway, pointed at the audience and screamed 'You're next!'

IOTBS proves it isn't paranoia if they are out to get you and plays on the notion of sleep as a portal to *real* nightmares. Siegel's taut direction overemphasises the normal, making the abnormal more horrifying. Miles' claustrophobia as the world closes in on him is expertly conveyed. Siegel's hard-nosed realism certainly rubbed off on his assistant, the great, troubled director Sam Peckinpah (*The Wild Bunch*), who has a small cameo.

The Incredible Shrinking Man (1957, USA) ★★★½

Dir: Jack Arnold; *Prod:* Albert Zugsmith; *Scr:* Richard Matheson, from his novel *The Shrinking Man*
St: Grant Williams, Randy Stuart, April Kent

A fantasy with a sf-nal sense of wonder. After his boat passes through a strange radioactive cloud, Scott Carey begins shrinking and doesn't stop. The film was a vehicle for spectacular size-based special effects (giant sets, camera tricks with giant cats, spiders, etc.), but it was invested with extra intelligence thanks to the talents of Matheson and Arnold. We care about Scott as he loses everything: status, self-respect, wife, home. His habitat reduces from house to doll's house to cellar (well-conceived as a totally alien environment), to the garden where he becomes too small to see but still defiantly asserts his humanity.

I Married A Monster From Outer Space (1958, USA) ★★★

Dir/Prod: Eugene Fowler, Jr; *Scr:* Louis Vittes
St: Tom Tryon, Gloria Talbott, Peter Baldwin

Getting drunk on your bachelor party is normal; getting taken over by an alien is just unlucky. That's what happens when Bill Farrell falls for the old 'body lying in the road' gag. 'Bill' marries poor Marge, who soon wonders why he has become an emotionless husk. She follows him into the forest and sees his true form as he enters his spaceship. She tries to escape by car but the police are aliens (did she not see *IOTBS*?). 'Bill' tells her that the aliens wish to breed with Earth women, as their female species has died out. Marge's doctor eventually believes her story. He assembles a group of local men with recently born children, who must *ergo* be human. The posse attack the aliens, and their dogs prove highly effective in ripping them apart. The real townsmen are found inside the ship and disconnected, causing the remaining aliens to jellify. As the invasion fleet flees Earth, Marge and Bill can look forward at last to reproducing with abandon.

IMAMFOS is an interesting, derivative film, riddled with 50s' skiffy. We're told the alien women died because of rays from their unstable sun! Judging by their menfolk, they probably expired from boredom. Why can't advanced invaders avoid blowing their cover so easily by failing to imitate human behaviour? This dopey lot wait around for a year to discover whether they can breed. Surely they'd just, er, have fun finding out? If they're able to exist on Earth in their plug-ugly alien form, why do they die the moment their human hosts are set free? And why do they bother creating facsimiles of men instead of just using their bodies? Answers on a postcard …

Stylishly directed, with a gritty tone and daring subtext of human/alien sexual relations, Fowler, Jr displays Fritz Lang's influence (he edited *The Woman In The Window* and *While The City Sleeps*) in touches of Langian noir: aliens' nightmarish features revealed in a flash of lightning and in a shop-window reflection; and 'Bill' murdering a prostitute who thinks he is a trick and strangling Marge's puppy when it won't stop barking at him (offscreen of course).

On The Beach (1959, USA) ★★★½

Dir/Prod: Stanley Kramer; *Scr:* John Paxter, from the novel by Nevil Shute
St: Gregory Peck, Ava Gardner, Fred Astaire, Anthony Perkins

Kramer's heavy but hypnotic parable divided critics and public alike. Some found it a timely and realistic warning of the dangers of nuclear war. Some found it maudlin and scientifically muddled. Many found it unpatriotic. The cast of heavyweights give a touch of class to a pregnant script that needlessly cushions armageddon by avoiding showing it. The people are just gone; no rotting bodies on the streets, no heaped cars on the highway. Australia awaits its fate as the last place on Earth hit by the fallout. US submarine Commander Towers falls for good-time gal Moira, but is guilt-ridden because of his deceased wife and kids. The best sequence is when the sub sets out to discover the source of a random radio signal from the San Diego area, but, in a wonderful piece of negative product placement, finds only a snagged Coke bottle desolately tapping a telegraph machine. In a balanced review, the *New York Daily News* prophesied that *OTB* heralded the '... eventual Communist enslavement of the entire human race', while Goddamn lily-livered pinko commsymp Linus Pauling called it the movie that could save the world. Well, it certainly did wonders for the song 'Waltzing Matilda'. Check it out next time on TV.

7: Damned Strange Odysseys (1960–1968)

> 'You can describe a typical fifties sf movie but there's no such thing as a typical sixties sf movie. Thematically, sf cinema diversified during this period and examined as a whole presents an eclectic range of subjects. It had also escaped, to some extent, from its B-movie status and many important directors tackled sf subjects … including Hitchcock, Kubrick, Godard, Frankenheimer, Truffaut, Losey, Lumet, Schaffner and Sturges, though often there would be a defensive announcement from the filmmaker concerned that his movie was not really science fiction but something, well, more important; this still goes on today.'
>
> John Brosnan (*The Primal Screen*)

Chaos Theory

The 60s saw cold war tensions escalate to almost the point of no return, and the Vietnam conflict become America's *bête noire*, even worse than Nagasaki and Hiroshima. Sf raged with debate about the contemporary world, which seemed more sf-nal than ever before. The previously close-knit sf community was divided, as magazines published lists of pro- and anti-Vietnam writers and rifts opened between those who couldn't forgive the other's position.

In 1963 President John F. Kennedy was assassinated in Texas, supposedly by lone gunman Lee Harvey Oswald. Suspicion grew that Kennedy's death was a political act perpetrated or aided by the secret services, to reassert a conservative hardline foreign-policy agenda. His successor Lyndon Johnson exacerbated the Vietnam debacle. A generation after the global insanity of WWII, a strong counterculture developed that sought to secure individual human rights. The hippy movement, mass demonstrations, civil unrest, racial tensions and progressive liberation marked the 60s as a turning point for paranoia. Attentions previously diverted to the skies were now focused upon the shady manoeuvrings of the state. Sf texts turned angry and postmodern, particularly the British New Wave mag *New Worlds*. Sf movies reflected the mood by diversifying from the standard 50s model into something far less predictable. The Russians had beaten the US into space, so space exploration movies weren't exactly in vogue. It was left to Stanley Kubrick to change and define the decade with two brilliant, epochal films: the first about the US threat to world peace and the second about the potential for human advancement, with a little help from our friends.

The Time Machine (1960, USA) ★★★

Dir/Prod: George Pal; *Scr:* David Duncan, from the novel by H.G. Wells
St: Rod Taylor, Yvette Mimieux, Alan Young

In the year 802,701 Victorian time traveller George finds society divided into two physical types: blond, elfin Eloi and subterranean hairy monster Morlocks. The Eloi sit around sunning themselves and the Morlocks feed on them. George develops a keen sense of injustice, fuelled by his desire for gorgeous nymphet Weena. He helps the Eloi rise up and overcome the Morlocks. After a brief visit to the past to tell his chums by the fireside, he hops back to the future with three unspecified books, presumably to educate his new people (Wellsian wish-fulfilment methinks).

Not in the same class as *WOTW*, Pal's second Wells adaptation has its moments (as the machine accelerates through time and the Sun wheels around the sky), but falls flat when it becomes a straightforward adventure romance. What about babies? Why are the Morlocks cannibalistic? Why … oh, forget it. It has plenty of charm, but Pal is only a workmanlike director and Aussie Hollywood hunk Taylor isn't exactly the image of a quintessentially English Victorian inventor.

La Jetée (1962, Fr) ★★★★

Dir/Scr: Chris Marker, *Prod:* Anatole Dauman
St: Hélène Chatelain, Davos Hanich, Jacques Ledoux, Jean
Négroni (voice)

Unique, beautiful 28-minute film that is actually a sequence of
still images and contains only one scene of movement. Its
story of a man unwittingly witnessing his own death forms the
basis of Terry Gilliam's *Twelve Monkeys* (1996). Every true sf
fan should track it down.

Dr. Strangelove Or: How I Learned To Stop Worrying And Love The Bomb (1963, UK/USA) ★★★★★

Dir/Prod: Stanley Kubrick; *Scr:* Kubrick, Terry Southern, Peter
George, from George's novel *Red Alert*
St: Peter Sellers, George C. Scott, Sterling Hayden, Keenan
Wynn

Burpelson Air Force Base. General Jack D. Ripper orders his
B-52 bombers to strike Russian targets in retaliation against a
nuclear attack. British officer Lionel Mandrake discovers there
is no Russian attack; Ripper has instigated armageddon as a
fait accompli, locked the base down and refuses to divulge the
recall codes. In the vast US War Room General Turgidson
urges President Muffley and the Chiefs Of Staff to take this
opportunity to neutralise the Russian threat. Muffley
disagrees, and phones Premier Kissoff with the bad news.
Much to Turgidson's disgust, Ambassador de Sadesky joins
them in the War Room. Kissoff says that if a single American
bomb is dropped, the Russian Doomsday Machine will
unleash a counterattack capable of destroying all human life.
Muffley gives the Russians the locations of the planes to shoot
them down. The army attacks Burpelson. After a bloody battle
the base is captured, but Ripper shoots himself. Mandrake has
worked out the codes but has to convince sceptical Colonel
'Bat' Guano to let him call the President. The recall is ordered.

One plane, the *Leper Colony*, flies on unaware, its communications damaged by a Russian missile. In the War Room Dr Strangelove, wheelchair-bound US weapons supremo and ex-Nazi, outlines a plan for the elite to live underground and breed, with a ratio of ten women to each man. Meanwhile, over its target, the *Leper Colony*'s bomb release mechanism is damaged, so redneck Major T.J. 'King' Kong rides it down like a bronco, thus triggering the Doomsday device.

Kubrick's savage satire on the futility of war retains its power to shock and awe. Recent events render timeless the film's mistrust of those who wield power over hardware that could end all our lives (Michael Moore's *Fahrenheit 9/11* is satirical and absurd, but it's a documentary). Sf's foremost auteur adapted George's novel as an all-out black comedy; severe on the US leadership, macho posturing and the male gender in general. He spares no political or military target (nor does he in *Paths Of Glory*, *A Clockwork Orange* and *Full Metal Jacket*). Sellers has three roles – stiff Brit gent Mandrake, ineffectual Muffley and mad scientist Strangelove – and is further off the leash than in *Lolita*. Merkin Muffley is mediocrity personified; both his names are slang for female pudenda. When de Sadesky and Turgidson come to blows, Muffley exclaims 'Gentlemen! You can't fight in here, this is the War Room.' Strangelove's appearance is brief but dynamite, his twisted persona a combination of Rotwang and Dr No. He is prone to involuntary outbursts ('Mein Führer!'), while his black-gloved hand grips his own throat and gives Nazi salutes. The lunatic has taken over the asylum, a swipe at US government hypocrisy that aided several Nazi rocket scientists to escape justice by seconding them after the war. Scott is a revelation as the pugnacious Turgidson, for whom even nuclear conflict has a positive spin – 'no more than 10 to 20 million killed, tops, depending on the breaks' – and de Sadesky's presence in the War Room is a greater outrage than bombing his country. Hayden is remarkable as the calm, unhinged Ripper, who, secure in his delusions that fluoridisation is a communist plot and women want to steal his precious bodily fluids, is unwilling to stick around to see the future his actions cause.

Everything about *Dr. Strangelove* feels right. The exaggerated tone works because the barbs are so sharp. Clever images and music complement acerbic dialogue; planes refuel in mid-air copulation to the strains of 'Try A Little Tenderness'; and the mushroom clouds billow as Vera Lynn sings 'We'll Meet Again'.

It radically divided opinion, being hailed as genius by liberals but vilified as unpatriotic by conservatives, as was the more sanitised *On The Beach*. It is one of the most important sf films and should be a set text in schools – a salutary warning to children of the dangers they might cause when pursuing a political or military career after failing to grow up.

Alphaville: Une Étrange Aventure De Lemmy Caution (1965, Fr.) ★

Dir/Scr: Jean-Luc Godard; *Prod:* André Michelin
St: Eddie Constantine, Anna Karina, Akim Tamiroff

Godard has made great films at the forefront of the European avant-garde since *À bout de Souffle* (1960). This pseudo-intellectual spoof isn't one of them. It's an alienating mishmash demonstrating Godard's indifference toward sf. Pretention dominates, as private eye Caution simply drives his Ford, crossing 'intersidereal space' to another planet, which looks suspiciously like Paris. He takes on Alphaville's supercomputer Alpha-6 using illogic (well, they got that right), and ends a mad scientist's totalitarian reign. I know I'm a philistine, but if you haven't seen it don't say I didn't warn you.

Daleks – Invasion Earth 2150 A.D. (1966, UK) ★★

Dir: Gordon Flemyng; *Prod:* Milton Subotsky, Max J. Rosenberg; *Scr:* Subotsky, from the TV series
St: Peter Cushing, Bernard Cribbins, Ray Brooks, Andrew Keir

Spin-off from the BBC's *Doctor Who* in which old adversaries the Daleks mine the Earth's core using controlled human slaves, and the Doctor and his assistants must save the day. Daleks resemble gliding pepperpots with fire grilles, sink plungers and flashing lights on their heads. They bark in grating electronic tones, slow-ly pro-noun-cing vow-els, and yell 'Ex-ter-minate!' a lot. They've managed to scare generations of British kids into watching them from behind chairs. Cushing is suitably eccentric, and the effects are variable. The final sequence when the model ship is overcome by magnetic force undoes most of the earlier good work as it wobbles into matchstick pylons and expires like a dud firework. Notable for the line 'We must avoid Watford. The place is crawling with Daleks.' (Well, it is if you're British.) This was the second Doctor Who film, which I prefer to the first, *Dr Who And The Daleks* (1965).

Fahrenheit 451 (1966, UK) ★★★

Dir: François Truffaut; *Prod:* Lewis M. Allen; *Scr:* Truffaut, Jean-Louis Richard, David Rudkin, Helen Scott, from the novel by Ray Bradbury
St: Oskar Werner, Julie Christie, Cyril Cusack, Anton Diffring

Montag is a fireman, but these firemen don't extinguish fires, they start them. Specifically, they burn books, because of the subversive social threat posed by them. Montag is troubled and his marriage is unhappy. After meeting Clarisse he joins her dissident group. Each member has memorised a work of their choice, to become, literally, a walking book. The title of the film refers to the temperature at which paper burns, and the firemen follow the Nazi doctrine of burning books to suppress undesirable cultures. Truffaut's film displays humanity and social conscience, in contrast to New Wave colleague Godard's postmodern autism. Truffaut confessed the film's faults in his admirably honest diaries from the period, but Bradbury's allegorical broadside against erosion of freedom and the rise of totalitarianism is fairly well served by this quirky adaptation. Some of its points are more relevant today than ever. Books are in danger of being usurped by mindless TV, and the lessons of the past are largely unheeded in the global headlong flight into nationalistic aggression. Watch and learn.

Fantastic Voyage (1966, USA) ★½

Dir: Richard Fleischer; *Prod:* Saul David; *Scr:* Harry Kleiner, from an adaptation by David Duncan of a story by Otto Klement and Jay Lewis (Jerome) Bixby
St: Stephen Boyd, Raquel Welch, Edmond O'Brien, Donald Pleasence

A submarine and crew are shrunk by a miniaturisation process and injected into a defecting Eastern bloc scientist dying from a blood clot in his brain. They have one hour to navigate his bloodstream and zap the clot with a laser. By the time the hour is up, the sub has been sabotaged and the crew, minus the dead commie (guess who), swim out through a tear duct before deminiaturising.

The basic problem with this premise is that the submarine's mass would cause it to drop through the man, the operating table and the floor. Still, science never was Hollywood's strong point. Isaac Asimov, author of the novelisation of the film, wrote in his memoirs that his daughter asked if the sub wouldn't just grow inside the scientist's head. He told her: '...you see that because you're smarter than the average Hollywood producer. After all, you're eleven.' The cast are given little to do, although Welch's assets are shown off nicely by a clinging wetsuit. The script is secondary to the effects, which ballooned the budget to $6.5 million. But the film made a profit, and Hollywood revisited miniaturisation in *Innerspace* (1987) and *Honey, I Shrunk The Kids* (1989) + sequels.

Barbarella (1968, Fr./It.) ★½

Dir: Roger Vadim; *Prod:* Dino De Laurentiis; *Scr:* Terry Southern, Vadim, Brian Degas, Jean-Claude Forest, from the book and comic strip by Forest

St: Jane Fonda, John Phillip Law, Anita Pallenberg, David Hemmings

As he'd done with former wife Brigitte Bardot, Vadim parades spouse Fonda's form in a movie with few other redeeming features. This psychedelic fantasy tosh is supposed to be tongue-in-cheek, but irritates rather than endears. Barbarella, a lone astronette searching for missing scientist Durand-Durand, has a series of 'adventures' that involve her getting semi-naked and sexually experimenting with various partners. Fair enough with Fonda in her gorgeous prime, but the film is a tease that promises without delivering, in every sense. Her journey consists of one silly, cloying episode after another; watching it feels like being trapped inside a pop-art womb, or the scientist's body from *Fantastic Voyage*. Save it for the drunken post-pub party.

Charly (1968, USA) **½

Dir/Prod: Ralph Nelson; *Scr:* Sterling Silliphant, from the novel *Flowers For Algernon* by Daniel Keyes
St: Cliff Robertson, Claire Bloom, Lilia Skala

Infuriating adaptation of Keyes' poignant story about a simpleton who is turned into a genius by a scientific experiment but the process then reverses. In the hands of a better director it could have been a dynamite film. The pathos of Charly's agonising descent into imbecility, all the worse because he's tasted what it's like to be superintelligent, is handled well and tugs the heartstrings. But the direction is stale, and the film never sparks into life around Robertson, who is the reason for watching. He was the driving force behind the project and his performance won a deserved Oscar, the only one to date for a lead actor in an sf film.

Planet Of The Apes (1968, USA) ***

Dir: Franklin J. Schaffner; *Prod:* Arthur P. Jacobs; *Scr:* Rod

Serling, Michael Wilson, from the novel *Monkey Planet* by Pierre Boulle
St: Charlton Heston, Roddy McDowall, Kim Hunter

A US space mission caught in a space/time anomaly crashes on an alien planet. The astronauts, led by Taylor, must try to survive in a world with inverted evolution – apes are educated and civilised, while humans are mute animals. Ape society doesn't take kindly to a human who can talk, and although his cause is championed by apemanitarian junior scientists Cornelius and Zira, chief scientist Dr Zaius wants Taylor dead. Badly.

Schaffner (*Patton*) directs with his usual macho punch and the film works best as straightforward, tough adventure. The apes are formidable creations; their entrance on horseback, hunting humans, is impressive. Co-screenwriter Serling created the classic sf TV series *The Twilight Zone* that ran between 1959 and 1963. The transference of human behavioural traits to apes allows him to spear home a few well-aimed misanthropic barbs. Some commentators have held that the film's success was evidence of a new Vietnam-cynical audience maturity, but I reckon the human condition criticism was simply missed by the majority. 'Whaddya mean? They're *apes*, man, they ain't supposed to be *us*!'

I like the film on an entertainment level, but I have one big problem with it that is shared by many. Megaspoiler coming up … at the end, Taylor finds the ruins of the Statue Of Liberty towering above a beach, proving that the alien planet is none other than far-future Earth. When I saw it, aged about 14 or 15, I must have missed something because I never for a second thought they were on an alien planet. I mean, there were humans and apes, and the latter spoke English; where the hell else would they be? But when people were going gaga about the cool ending – 'Jeez, they were really on *Earth* all along! It blew my mind!' – I wondered if there was something wrong with me for not feeling it. UK's Channel 5 obviously didn't feel it – a trailer for an upcoming screening included the final Statue scene!

POTA's resounding success ($33 million in the US) had generated four sequels by 1973 (*Beneath ...*, *Escape From ...*, *Conquest Of ...*, and *Battle For ...*), plus a spin-off TV series, a Marvel comic and, so far thankfully only one 'reimagining'. Give it a rest now guys willya, huh? Please?

2001: A SPACE ODYSSEY (1968, UK) *****

Dir/Prod: Stanley Kubrick; *Scr:* Kubrick, Arthur C. Clarke, from Clarke's story *The Sentinel*
St: Keir Dullea, Gary Lockwood, William Sylvester

The Dawn Of Man. Early hominids eke out a precarious existence, sheltering in a cave and trying to survive. Suddenly in their midst appears a giant black monolith. An ape touches it, then intuits how to kill a rival with an animal bone. Human evolution has been kick-started. A few million years later a similar monolith is unearthed on the Moon, and sends a piercing signal towards Jupiter. Eighteen months afterwards the spacecraft Discovery heads for Jupiter, but its crew are killed by malfunctioning ship computer HAL-9000. The sole survivor, Bowman, dismantles HAL's higher brain functions and continues the mission alone. The Discovery encounters a vast monolith near Jupiter. Bowman investigates in a pod and passes through the Star Gate, an awesome trip that overloads his senses and accelerates his aging process. In a sterile environment, probably created from his own mind, he nears the end of his life. Another small monolith appears at the foot of his deathbed. He is 'reborn' as a foetal lifeforce, a Star Child, overlooking Earth.

The best *science* fiction movie ever made. Kubrick's masterpiece changed people's perceptions of sf film's potential, and was its own evolutionary leap in sophistication. Although based on Clarke's story, it is Kubrick's movie. He created cinema's most rational sense of wonder not by resorting to generic formula, but by transcending it. He trusted the audience to follow as he tackled the great metaphysical questions: the nature of human and artificial intelligence; of God and the infinite Universe, and alien (divine?) intervention in human evolution. He made no compromise to traditional film narrative; of 137 minutes, only 40 contained dialogue. There is a cold, cerebral tone, a deliberately slow pace, and no real protagonist or familiar structure. Space is soundless save for monotonous breathing, one aspect of Kubrick's complete scientific accuracy. The realistic sets included a $750,000 moving wheel to facilitate the illusion of zero-gravity exercise. For the effects team, including Douglas Trumbull and Wally Veevers, nothing short of perfection was required. They innovated and experimented with a phenomenal range of models, optical processes, mattes, projections and camera motion control systems, and won Kubrick his only Oscar (Stuart Freeborn's uncannily realistic ape outfits were beaten to the MakeUp award by *Planet Of The Apes*).

2001 is a majestic, sweeping, portentous epic spanning mankind's journey from prehistory to the space age, as the hominids learn to dominate their environment under the watchful presence of the monolith, space stations spin in slow-motion majesty to Strauss and Debussy waltzes, and Bowman plunges into a mind-blowing array of dizzying colour-saturated stellar imagery.

Critical reaction was hostile, but a large cult following has deified it. The edit that spans millennia by match-cutting a whirling bone with a tumbling orbital bomb has become as celebrated as *Lawrence Of Arabia*'s match strike/rising sun. Bowman's dismantling of HAL's 'brain' as it begs him to stop and sings *Daisy* until it winds down is one of cinema's greatest scenes.

Kubrick's contention seems to be that mankind's potential is unknowable, possibly limitless, but can only be achieved by constantly aiming for higher goals, whether setting them ourselves or having them set for us by advanced intelligences. *2001* is Pure Cinema; there is no other experience like it. Lobby hard to see it in 70mm on a big screen, as Kubrick meant it to be seen, the only way to appreciate fully its towering, unparalleled achievement.

6: Dystopia, Dattopia (1970–1976)

'[1970s] Science fiction has become much more seriously intentioned and, unfortunately, more pretentious. Much like the Western during the fifties and sixties, science fiction pictures like The Terminal Man, *... A* Clockwork Orange, Silent Running, *and even the fatuous ones like* Soylent Green, *pretend to greater themes ... Many people simply do not enjoy seeing science fiction pictures.'*

John Carpenter (Writer/Director)

Politics, Sex, Drugs And Rock 'N' Roll

Despite the greatest example of sf becoming fact, the US Moon landing in 1969, the most prevalent themes in 70s sf cinema were (lack of) free will, totalitarianism, ugliness, cynicism and violence. The world was a very different place than at the dawn of the 60s: older, wiser, angrier. Vietnam raged on. President Nixon was exposed as a liar and a thief by *Washington Post* journalists but resigned before being impeached. Hollywood had also changed. The old studio guard had been usurped by young longhairs from the independent scene. Films like *Easy Rider, M.A.S.H., Midnight Cowboy* and *The Wild Bunch* catapulted counterculture into profitability. They opened up new vistas of sex, violence and social commentary, and studios were more sympathetic to 'difficult' narratives driven by a negative philosophy about the modern world. For the first half of the decade, most sf films posited dystopian futures irreparably damaged by the present: repressive regimes; decadent societies; corrupt corporations; population control/explosion; Earth's resources squandered or abused; and other planets casually bombed. Everything was going to hell in a handbasket, although in 1977 the situation would be totally turned around.

The Andromeda Strain (1970, USA) ★★★

Dir/Prod: Robert Wise; *Scr:* Nelson Gidding, from the novel by Michael Crichton
St: Arthur Hill, David Wayne, James Olson

Slow-paced sf/horror that updates Quatermass's space virus to New Mexico, where a crashed satellite releases a plague that decimates a small town's population, except for two survivors: a wino and a baby. If the world's top scientists can't develop a cure from their immunity, Earth's fate is in the balance. The secret underground government laboratory, the Wildfire Complex, houses the technology to crack the problem, but the virus cannot be contained, and Wildfire is programmed to self-destruct if the virus is released.

Technology and disaster are Crichton's signature obsessions, with human characters often relegated to second billing. With Wise at the helm, though, this is tense and atmospheric, one of the best movies from a Crichton source.

THX 1138 (1970, USA) ★★★★

Dir: George Lucas; *Prod:* Francis Ford Coppola, Lawrence Sturhahn; *Scr:* Lucas, Walter Murch, from a story by Lucas
St: Robert Duvall, Maggie McOmie, Don Pedro Colley, Donald Pleasence

Earth's surface is a radioactive wasteland, so humanity lives a subterranean existence. Everyone wears white overalls and has shaven heads, even women. Sex is outlawed and libidos are kept in check by daily drug rations. 'God' is on hand in auto-mated booths, spouting recorded platitudes. Leather-clad, chrome-faced robot police have little to do. No one has names as we know them. LUH 3417 and her partner, nuclear worker THX 1138, skip their drug intake and have intercourse. He becomes incapable of doing his job and is responsible for a major accident. She becomes pregnant, punishable by death. He is held in a featureless white prison, from which he simply walks away. He steals a motorbike and is pursued through tunnels by the robot police before they stop the chase because the budget has run out. Finally, THX ascends a ladder to the surface and discovers the Big Lie as he emerges into the light of a glorious sunrise.

Before he found the Force, Student George made a *science fiction* film, and a very good one. He expanded his original graduation film *THX 2238 4EB* with help from Francis Ford Coppola's Zoetrope company. It's tempting to regard it as the two sides of George battling for supremacy. The first is clever dystopian sf in the grand tradition of *1984*, *Brave New World* and Zamyatin's *We*, while the other is a chase romp with funny-looking robots. The story wins no prizes for originality, but the style is formidable, with crisp, sterile visuals and a superb sound collage by Walter Murch (who did great work on Coppola's *The Conversation* and *Apocalypse Now*, which Lucas was to have directed). Layers of impressionistic details flesh out the reality of THX's world. Unfortunately, Lucas' sly swipe at capitalism, censorship and repressive politics died at the box office. When he couldn't beat 'em, he joined 'em with a vengeance. His teen flick *American Graffiti* became one of the most profitable gross-to-budget sleeper hits ever, and gave him the clout to embark upon his space opera for ten year olds, *Star Wars*.

Lately, Megalomaniac George has been busily integrating digital effects into *THX* for its DVD release, otherwise known as meddling the hell with it. If you own a video or, better, a laserdisc of the original, hold onto it – if MG has his way, the original version may never make it to the surface. George, this may be your movie, but yet again it's our nostalgia you're stomping into the Skywalker ranch dust, Goddammit.

A Clockwork Orange (1971, UK) ★★★★

Dir/Prod: Stanley Kubrick; *Scr:* Kubrick, from the novel by Anthony Burgess
St: Malcolm McDowell, Patrick Magee, Adrienne Corri

Alex and his Droogs Pete, Georgie and Dim drink milk-plus in the Korova before a night of ultraviolence and 'the old in-out, in-out'. That is, they get high, beat up a drunk, ambush a rival gang and drive a stolen sports car to a country house. There they assault left-wing writer Frank Alexander and rape his wife, to the strains of 'Singin' In The Rain'. On their next outing, Alex kills a female sculptor but his Droogs bottle him and leave him for the police. After two years in jail, Alex volunteers for the controversial Ludovico Technique, to cure his psychopathic tendencies. He is drugged and forced to watch scenes of torture and murder while listening to his beloved Beethoven's Ninth Symphony until even the thought of violence (or Beethoven) makes him puke. Upon his release his parents disown him, he is beaten up by Georgie and Dim, now policemen, and taken in by Alexander, now a widower, who sees him as a victim of the state. When Alex takes a bath and warbles 'Singin' In The Rain,' Alexander realises who he really is. He plays Beethoven loudly, and Alex jumps out of a first-floor window. In hospital, the Home Office Minister cuts a deal with Alex to avoid bad press. Alex fantasises deliriously about sex and violence. He's 'cured'.

One of the most controversial films ever, *ACO* is a satire that blitzes its targets but became a victim of its own success. Much of its mystique is down to Kubrick's withdrawal of it from public viewing in Britain in 1974 following hostile press, tales of copycat rapes and violence, and death threats. It was only re-released in 2000, a year after his death. Although reviled for celebrating violence and rape (the opposite of the intent), and its then-extreme violence and full-frontal nudity, Luis Buñuel called it '... the only movie about what the modern world really means'. It asks whether free will should be removed from violent criminals for the greater social good, and is a 'deprogrammed' individual still human? That Kubrick and Burgess argued not outraged the Conservative right, who are roundly lampooned. Alex is proposed as a victim: he loves Beethoven, and were he not from the wrong side of the social divide, he may have become more like his namesake, Alexander. Burgess emphasised the theological point:'If we are going to love mankind, we will have to love Alex as a not unrepresentative member of it.' He wrote the novel in alcoholic anger after a vicious assault on his wife by four AWOL WWII American soldiers.

Always ahead of his time, Kubrick's cartoonlike set-pieces inspired Tarantino, Oliver Stone, etc. In fact, scenes like Alex killing the cat-woman with a big pop-art penis sculpture, or having speeded-up sex with two schoolgirls *á la* Benny Hill, are high-camp slapstick. The film's major fault is that Kubrick megaphones every point even though he's standing next to us. His caricatures are hyper-exaggerated, like a TV sitcom. Underpinning every frame of his films is a misanthropic wish that man could be less instinctual ape and more refined intellect, yet the paradox is it's the apes he makes movies about. His magnifying glass clinically scrutinises man's flaws, and only in *2001* does he see a positive way forward. In fact, he had not read the last chapter of *ACO*, which saw Alex settle down with a family, because it was cut from the US edition. I think we can be thankful for that.

As ever, it's Kubrick's imagery that stays with you. The Allen Jones-style female furniture in the Korova; the white overalls, false noses, codpieces and black bowler hats of the Droogs; extreme close-ups of eyes and faces; slow- and fast-motion, fisheye lenses, pop-art production design ... all extremely influential pillars of the 70s *zeitgeist*. McDowell was chosen because of his role in Lindsay Anderson's *If...* and is superb. Warren Clarke, who plays Dim, is a familiar figure on British TV in the police drama *Dalziel & Pascoe*. Alexander's assistant was none other than Dave Prowse, later to become Darth Vader.

Slaughterhouse Five (1971, USA) ★★½

Dir: George Roy Hill; *Prod:* Paul Monash; *Scr:* Stephen Geller, from the novel by Kurt Vonnegut, Jr
St: Michael Sachs, Ron Leibman, Eugene Roche, Valerie Perrine

Vonnegut's surreal, oblique style stretches the fabric of sf; unfortunately, the film never quite captures the right tone. Hapless Billy Pilgrim has come 'unstuck' in time, and relives his life from the WWII firebombing of Dresden where he was a prisoner of war, to his future, caged with Hollywood glam girl Montana Wildhack as a zoo exhibit on alien planet Tralfamadore. Billy's trip is an interior one (as Newton's may be in *The Man Who Fell To Earth*), and the elliptical time-shifting narrative works better in the novel. The film has merit but reduces Vonnegut's sharp multiple meanings to mulch. One of the problems with sf film is that when it shows everything literally (i.e., most of the time), this removes the vital function of our imagination. Vonnegut needs to be read and not seen.

Silent Running (1972, USA) ★½

Dir: Douglas Trumbull; *Prod:* Michael Gurskoff; *Scr:* Michael Cimino, Deric Washburn, Steven Bochco, from a story by Trumbull
St: Bruce Dern, Cliff Potts, Ron Rifkin

Special effects wunderkind Trumbull made his directing debut with sf's first eco-fable, but despite its cult following I find it tedious and maudlin. Kubrick's influence didn't rub off – its science, character motivation and plot development are garbled and unbelievable. I can't empathise with protagonist Lowell, who kills his colleagues to save a bunch of plants. Its eco-friendly hippy sensibility is annoying, backed up by some cringeworthy music. Most people's interest focuses on the three mini-robots, Huey, Dewey and Louie, who were played by amputees walking on their hands.

Solaris [Solyaris] (1972, USSR) ★★★★

Dir: Andrei Tarkovsky; *Scr:* Tarkovsky, Friedrich Gorenstein, from the novel by Stanislaw Lem
St: Donatis Banionis, Natalya Bondarchuk, Yuri Jarvet

Scientist Kris Kelvin is sent to a research station orbiting the ocean planet Solaris, to investigate strange happenings and pychological problems among the crew. Gibaryan has killed himself and the others are scared and secretive. Kelvin soon finds why: when he wakes, his wife Hari is by his side. But Hari committed suicide years ago.

Labelled 'The Russian *2001*', this 165-minute, ponderous gem is a metaphysical meditation on identity, loneliness and nostalgia. *CFQ* called it '… a humanistic response to Kubrick's vision of technological aridity.' When Kelvin kills 'Hari' by ejecting her into space, she simply reappears. Nor can she kill herself (again) by swallowing liquid oxygen. Like Rachael in *Blade Runner* she must somehow come to terms with being both real and artificial, and Kelvin has to fathom the purpose of the sentient planet's 'companion' constructs. Visual poet Tarkovsky amplifies Lem's use of outer space as a metaphor for inner space. The funereal pace will alienate 90 per cent of modern viewers, but *Solaris* is a must for true sf fans, as is Tarkovsky's other oblique, elliptical sf film *Stalker* (1979), based on the excellent novel *Roadside Picnic* by Arkady and Boris Strugatsky.

A 2002 remake of *Solaris* was adapted and directed by Steven Soderbergh, and produced by James Cameron. It stars George Clooney and Natascha McElhone, and is a worthy if insubstantial successor, played out as an sf romance.

Sleeper (1973, USA) ★★★

Dir: Woody Allen; *Prod:* Jack Grossberg; *Scr:* Allen, Marshall Brickman
St: Allen, Diane Keaton, John Beck

After 200 years in cryogenic suspension, Miles Monroe is revived and inadvertently becomes embroiled in a revolution to overthrow America's totalitarian regime. He hides by impersonating a robot butler in the home of hopeless poet Luna. When the revolutionaries bomb the regime's Leader, Miles and Luna must steal the remains – his nose – before the authorities can clone it. This pacy, slapstick spoof engages the brain and tickles the rib in equal measure.

Westworld (1973, USA) ★★★

Dir/Scr: Michael Crichton; *Prod:* Paul N. Lazarus III
St: Yul Brynner, Richard Benjamin, James Brolin

Futuristic theme park Delos has three artificial environments, populated by artificial people, where wealthy tourists can act out their vicarious fantasies: Romanworld, Medievalworld and Westworld. Two guys enjoy their time whoring, drinking and shooting robot cowboys in the old Wild West … until the robots start shooting back.

Silly but magnetically watchable trash-thriller that explains nothing, just gets on with the action. Why do the robots malfunction? No idea, they just do. Why are the robots distinguishable from humans because their hands aren't perfect? Eldon Tyrell wouldn't let that happen. It's as dumb as saying the Disneyland guys just can't get Mickey's ears right. The pixellated POV as the gunslinger chases its human target is an early and effective use of the device. The character, played by Brynner as an android simulacrum of his role in *The Magnificent Seven* is the best thing about the film. His dogged tracking of Benjamin, even with his face eaten off by acid, is a memorable foretaste of the Terminator's single-minded pursuit.

Soylent Green (1973, USA) ★★½

Dir: Richard Fleischer; *Prod:* Walter Selzer, Russell Thacher; *Scr:* Stanley R. Greenberg, from the novel *Make Room! Make Room!* by Harry Harrison
St: Charlton Heston, Edward G. Robinson, Leigh Taylor-Young

Detective Frank Thorn investigates the murder of the chief of Soylent Corp. Soylent makes a soya/lentil product that feeds the New York metropolis, pop. 40 million. When Thorn digs too far, he finds that Soylent's food isn't exactly what it's claimed to be.

'Soylent Green is people!' is an sf catchphrase up there with the best, but its founding principle is sheer skiffy. If the oceans are dry (which would not only mean no population explosion, but no population at all) and the world is bursting at the seams, how else is everyone going to be fed? The novel's hard-hitting treatise about world overpopulation is strained into a standard-issue detective/conspiracy story. Robinson is underused but brings a dignity to his last role (he died just after shooting). Heston fought to bring the novel to the screen, and plays … Charlton Heston, just like always. Like *Westworld*, *SG* was highly profitable, which is pretty amazing considering the subject. Try doing something like it now without losing your shirt.

DARK STAR (1974, USA) ★★★★★

Dir: John Carpenter; *Prod:* Jack H. Harris; *Scr:* Carpenter, Dan O'Bannon
St: Brian Narelle, Dre Pahich, Cal Kuniholm, O'Bannon

The *Dark Star's* mission to destroy 'unstable planets' has been dogged by bad luck. Commander Powell was electrocuted in his chair, a radiation leak forced the crew into unsuitable quarters, and the ship's entire supply of toilet paper has been lost. Doolittle, Boiler and Pinback spend their lives squabbling, while Talby never leaves the observation dome, hoping to realise his life's ambition to see the fabled Phoenix asteroids that 'circle the Universe every 1.23 trillion years'. Pinback relates a story that he is actually maintenance engineer Bill Froug, who donned the suit of the real Pinback after his suicide leap into a vat of liquid oxygen, but couldn't work the helmet radio to tell anyone. Doolittle moans that Pinback told them this four years ago, but Boiler maintains it was *four* years ago. The computer's female purr announces they're approaching an energy field similar to the one that killed Commander Powell. They surround the ship with a stasis field while the force passes. Later, they ignore a report on damage to the emergency airlock. Pinback is unhappy about cleaning out the resident pet alien, a rotund, squeaking, moronic vegetable. When it attacks and chases him into an elevator shaft it becomes a life-or-death struggle. He finally shoots it with a tranquilliser dart, which punctures it like a balloon.

The ship arrives at the next planet for destruction. Talby is suited up in the airlock, trying to locate the problem, but steps into the beam of a communications laser. The bomb drop sequence malfunctions, creating hysterical panic. The bomb peevishly refuses an order to abort its countdown. Doolittle revives Commander Powell from cryogenic suspension. Powell only wants to talk about the Dodgers, but he eventually advises Doolittle to teach the bomb phenomenology. Doolittle exits the ship and persuades the bomb that it has no objective proof that its sensory data is correct, therefore it must not destruct in case the order was false. The bomb retreats inside the ship. When Doolittle opens the emergency airlock, Talby is ejected into space. As Doolittle jets after him, Boiler and Pinback listen in horror as the bomb elucidates its new-found self-awareness, concluding: 'Let there be light.' After the explosion, Doolittle finds a makeshift board among the ship debris and surfs towards the planet, while Talby drifts into the strange, glowing Phoenix asteroids, destined to accompany them forever on their journey around the Universe.

Carpenter had already won an Oscar, for his and Jim Rokos' 1970 short *The Resurrection Of Bronco Billy*. His graduation film, an affectionate riposte to *2001*, *Dr. Strangelove* and *Star Trek*, was originally called *The Electric Dutchman*, as a tribute to Philip K. Dick. It was a true labour of love: Carpenter directed, produced and scored, while co-writer O'Bannon was responsible for on-set special effects, set design and editing, and was hilarious as whining slacker Pinback.

They spent two years battling to raise cash to expand the 50-minute student film, and upgrade 16mm footage to 35mm. A $10,000 donation from fellow student Jonathan Kaplan was spent shooting the elevator shaft scenes, as the old ship sets were long gone. Later, broke again, they handed ownership to independent producer Jack Harris to fund extra shots and postproduction. By 1974 the crew finally had a finished film, but they were exhausted and dispirited. Harris sold the movie to distributors Bryanston, whose 1975 cinema release let it die a quiet death. Carpenter and O'Bannon have described the experience as the worst of their lives.

The zero-budget effects included some fine work: animation by Bob Greenberg, models by Greg Jein, computer readouts by John Wash, paintings by Jim Danforth, opticals by Bill Taylor and designs by Ron Cobb. The alien looked remarkably like a painted beach ball with claws – which it was. The sequence when Pinback hangs in a shaft being menaced by the ridiculous alien and a descending elevator was a triumph of ingenuity: O'Bannon lay on a (sometimes) hidden plank in a horizontal set, and the 'elevator' was pushed along on wheels. Carpenter's electronic score was augmented by classical and country and western music; the title song *Benson, Arizona* was written by Bill Taylor. The real Bill Froug was a screenwriting tutor at USC. By mid-1973 the principals were barely on speaking terms. Carpenter refused O'Bannon the co-director or co-producer credit he felt he deserved. The poster tag line read 'Bombed out in space with a spaced-out bomb', and the film is a reflection of its time: the nihilistic humour and the disaffected, hirsute crew are pure 70s underground. It's existential sf; as Carpenter said, '*Waiting For Godot* in outer space.'

I saw *Dark Star* on TV in 1977 (two days after *Silent*

Running; it was everything *SR* was not), and no sf film before or since has had as profound and devastating an effect. Not *Alien*, nor *Blade Runner*. For me it was and is a perfect synthesis of wonder, humour, intellect and melancholia, and a testament to the genius of its creators.

Rollerball (1975, USA) ★★★½

Dir/Prod: Norman Jewison; *Scr:* William Harrison, from his story, *Roller Ball Murders*
St: James Caan, Maud Adams, John Houseman, John Beck

In 2018, nations have been replaced by Corporations in charge of the world's resources. Rollerball, a gladiatorial game played in a banked arena by teams of skaters and bikers, is used as a means of social control. Jonathan E, captain of the mighty Houston team, refuses an order to retire because he is becoming bigger than the game. The Energy Corporation relaxes the rules in an attempt to get rid of him, but after the carnage of the no-rules final, Jonathan stands unbowed on the corpse-littered track as the fans howl his name and the thwarted executives glower.

An unsubtle warning about dehumanisation and corporate power, *Rollerball* is intriguing but uneven. The game sequences are so exciting that the drama pales by comparison. Caan's gruff, monosyllabic Jonathan has almost everything a man could want, so his dogged quest to reclaim his ex-wife from a corporate executive comes across as petulant self-indulgence. His life off the track is so full of ennui that it's difficult to care about him. Only Moonpie (Beck) seems to really love life, and in a memorable scene he is singled out, surrounded and slain in slow-motion by the fearsome Tokyo team. The future society's selfish hedonism is nicely captured in a party scene in which the guests torch tall trees with flame-throwers, but there is a skiffy sequence with Ralph Richardson as the keeper of a temperamental liquid computer called Zero (strange how most 70s sf movies have similar elements). The main attraction is the action, intoxicatingly set to Bach's *Toccata in E Minor*.

Rollerball was widely criticised for its violence and lack of plot but it's a valuable sf film, and a masterpiece compared to John McTiernan's 2000 remake.

A Boy And His Dog (1975, USA) ★★½

Dir: L.Q. Jones; *Prod:* Alvy Moore; *Scr:* Jones, from the novella by Harlan Ellison
St: Don Johnson, Susann Benton, Alvy Moore, Jason Robards

In post-holocaust Arizona, Vic and Blood scavenge the desert. Blood sniffs out girls for Vic to rape, as long as Vic finds food. Theirs is a strange partnership, not least because they communicate telepathically and because Blood is a dog. Blood detects a girl who, to Vic's surprise, is sexually responsive to him. A band of rovers attack, and Blood is injured. The girl, Quilla June, escapes. Vic follows her downunder to Topeka, an odd, isolated community. He has been lured there to impregnate women (the men are impotent), but only by sperm donation. He is then to be killed. Rebels try to overthrow the ruling committee, and Vic and Quilla June escape. Up above, Blood is starving to death. Quilla June wants Vic to leave him and go with her. Later, Vic and the rejuvenated Blood walk off into the distance, alone.

Blood's punchline that Quilla June had 'great taste' upset a lot of people, particularly feminists who deplored the perceived misogyny of the novella and the film. Ellison vehemently denied the charge, but admitted being uncomfortable about the film's final scene. Jones was a character actor who appeared in Peckinpah Westerns and set up a production company with fellow actor Moore. Ellison had been engaged to write the script but encountered writers' block for the first time, so Jones wrote it himself. The Topeka sequence is a classic case of 70s oddball skiffy theatre, but the rest has a sf unity of idea and execution that merits its deserved cult following.

The Man Who Fell To Earth (1976, UK/USA) ★★★½

Dir: Nicolas Roeg; *Prod:* Michael Deeley, Barry Spikings; *Scr:*
Paul Mayersberg, from the novel by Walter S. Tevis
St: David Bowie, Candy Clark, Rip Torn, Buck Henry

A dense, elliptical space oddity about an emaciated alien who
lands on Earth to find the means of building a spaceship to
rescue his people from their dying planet. Or maybe it's a
parable about a tortured rock star (Bowie playing himself?)
living in a bubble of drugs, self-loathing and hangers-on. Or,
as Peter Nicholls suggests, a parallel with mega-rich paranoid
recluse Howard Hughes. The alien, Thomas Jerome Newton,
founds a multimillion dollar corporation, World Enterprises,
but becomes sidetracked by booze and television. Easily
manipulated by the sharks that surround him, his mission is
never accomplished as his life goes to the dogs just like a native
Earthman's. Roeg (*Performance, Don't Look Now*) fashioned a
strange, downbeat art film from Tevis' linear novel, with few
overtly sf-nal elements. He invests the material with heavy
symbolism (the fall of Icarus) and the meaninglessness of
modern life. If Newton is an ET, he's the first to be taken over
by us instead of vice-versa, and he never gets to phone home.

5: The Biggest Bang (1977–1982)

'Steven Spielberg and George Lucas have changed the way stories are told for the first time since Homer. They're told now like amusement park rides.'

John Milius (Director/Screenwriter)

Enter The Movie Brats

Without warning, the wave of difficult 70s dystopias was buried under a sugar avalanche, triggered by two film school geeks who turned the movie industry on its head. Spielberg and Lucas hauled sf into the mainstream, a development I have plenty of reservations about. They made 'em efficiently, and the returns were beyond belief. Separately or together, Spielberg and Lucas made the top-grossing films of 1976, 1977, 1980, 1981, 1982, 1983, 1993, 1998 and 1999, those movies alone totalling over $3 billion in America!

Science Fiction, Fantasy, Father George And Uncle Steven

Lucas and Spielberg created an sf/fantasy chimera to rule a vast empire. But we already know that sf + fantasy = skiffy. Adult sf became marginalised and the movie brats gave themselves power over life and death. In *Star Wars* Father George couldn't bring himself to *kill* Obi-Wan Kenobi, he just sent him to a special FX dimension to chip in from the wings. Ditto Yoda. In *Close Encounters of the Third Kind* Uncle Steven's unaged WWII pilots and abductees were cared for by nice spindly aliens whom we just knew hadn't administered any disgusting anal probes. He killed off his cuddly little E.T. hero

… nope, just kidding, here he is again. Result: millions of tears and dollars successfully jerked. Soft toys were shifted by the mothershipload, begetting the dreadful teddybear Ewoks. Soon stiffs were being brought back by time travel (Lois Lane in *Superman*); glowing balls (*Starman*); re-energised life-force (*Star Trek III*); or simply resuscitated before they're too dead (*The Abyss*).

Of course, power becomes its own justification, and the more power you have the more justified you are. Remember the scene in *Star Wars* – pardon me, *Star Wars Episode IV: A New Hope* – where Han Solo boasts that the *Millennium Falcon* '…made the Kessel run in less than 12 parsecs'? Father George didn't care that a parsec is a unit of distance, not time. He maintains he *knew* but doesn't have to explain himself, and that's the problem nailed right there. Now he's so far up his own, er, universe that he's altering his films against the wishes of millions of fans. Uncle Steven was so upset at having to remove the song 'When You Wish Upon A Star' from *CE3K* that he brought out a Special Edition with it reinstated. After Kubrick's death (such a pity *Stanley* couldn't be brought back), he reduced *A.I.* to a fairytale that abandoned sf to recycle Pinocchio.

But Godhood is catching, in more ways than one. Ridley Scott and James Cameron are among those with the clout to release preferred editions of their work, so for those of us who prefer the original cut of *Blade Runner*, that's tough. Godhood has become one of the principal themes of skiffy. The last two instalments in the *The Matrix* trilogy sacrificed the brilliance of the first at Father George's new age altar. Frank Herbert's great novel *Dune* was another victim. *Star Trek* embraced similar braindead mysticism; in three of the first five films the Enterprise crew met various forms of 'God'. Maybe it's time the genre was renamed Antiscience Fiction, or Theological Fantasy.

The catch-22 is that Lucas and Spielberg galvanised studio activity in the sf market. Had they not made such incredible sums of money, some of the best sf movies would never have been made. Conversely, we wouldn't have had to endure a barrage of big-budget sf lamebrains, and we may have had more outstanding films questioning social values and provoking thought. Like mobile phones, their omnipotence pressed the dumbing-down accelerator to the floor, yet most people can't imagine life without them.

Star Wars Episode IV: A New Hope (1977, USA) ★★★★

Dir/Scr: George Lucas; *Prod:* Gary Kurtz
St: Mark Hamill, Harrison Ford, Carrie Fisher, Alec Guinness

Princess Leia Organa's ship is swallowed by an Imperial Battlecruiser and the evil Darth Vader accuses her of belonging to the Rebel Alliance. Two 'droids', C-3PO and R2-D2, flee in an escape pod to the desert planet, Tatooine. They are captured by Jawa scavengers and sold to Luke Skywalker, a youth who'd rather be fighting the Galactic Empire than working on his uncle's farm. After discovering a distress message hidden in the R-2 droid, from the Princess to someone called Obi-Wan, Luke seeks out local recluse Ben Kenobi. Ben claims to be a fabled Jedi Knight, exponents of a mystical martial art/religion known as the Force. He says Luke's dead father was also a Jedi, betrayed by Vader who turned to the Dark Side. Leia's message asks him to deliver R2 to her father, the Emperor on Alderaan. Luke returns home to find his aunt and uncle have been murdered by Stormtroopers hunting the droids.

At Mos Eisley spaceport, Luke and Ben charter the *Millennium Falcon*, captained by mercenary Han Solo and crewed by Chewbacca, a giant fur-covered Wookie. They are soon chased by Imperial fighters. After escaping into hyper-space, Han is contemptuous of Luke's efforts to learn the Force from Ben. Meanwhile aboard the Death Star, a battle station the size of a moon, Vader punishes Leia's refusal to reveal the location of the Rebel Alliance by destroying Alderaan. The *Millennium Falcon* is captured by the Death Star. After escaping within, Luke and Han rescue Leia. Kenobi faces Vader in a lightsaber duel and, when struck down, disappears.

After a pitched battle, the others fight their way aboard the *Falcon* and take off.

At the Rebel base, Alliance leaders study the Death Star plans hidden in the R2 droid. Their attack strategy uses swift X-Wing fighters to deliver a proton bomb into the reactor core, but chances of success are negligible. Worse, the *Falcon* has been tracked by the Death Star, so failure will result in destruction. To Leia's disgust, Solo takes his money and leaves. Rebel fighters sustain heavy losses, until Luke is their final hope. Vader is about to blast him when Solo intervenes, sending Vader's ship spinning into space. Luke hears Ben telling him to trust the Force, and disengages his targeting computer. His instinctive shot is successful and the Death Star is destroyed. At the Rebel base, crowds cheer as Leia bestows the heroes with medals.

'A long time ago in a galaxy far, far away' and 'May the Force be with you' are hardwired into our collective psyche. *Star Wars* is the biggest sf movie phenomenon ever, a high-quality, low-genre space opera that exploded out of nowhere. *2001* was an important landmark, but *Star Wars* was pop sf; Beatlemania to the power of X. People had never before queued around the block for an sf film, nor seen one umpteen times, nor devoured mountains of merchandise faster than it could be churned out.

Its first run took over $215million, against a cost of $11 million. These grosses catapulted sf from pariah to Saviour Of Hollywood as the studios fell over each other to rush sf into production. This was ironic because sf was merely the vehicle Lucas chose for a saga based upon the timeless myths chronicled in Joseph Campbell's book *The Hero With A Thousand Faces*. Archetypal hero Skywalker's triumph against impossible odds to rescue the Princess and save the Universe is a compendium of cultural myths and fairy tales: David vs Goliath; Arthurian legend (Knights Of The Round Table, Merlin the sorceror and the boy who would be King); the Samurai code; *The Wizard Of Oz*; Kurosawa's *The Hidden Fortress*, etc. After *THX 1138*, Lucas did not want to make niche sf that no one saw, so he made *SW* for the young of all ages. It was great fun, and gave people something to make the world palatable again. But it had its detractors. John Brosnan wrote: 'It was mindless ... Lucas had taken sf cinema out of the hands of adults and into the nursery where it has tended to remain ever since.' Paul Schrader (writer of *Taxi Driver*) said that *Star Wars* '... ate the heart and soul of Hollywood. It created the big-budget comic book mentality.'

I agree, so here's a shock: as brain-on-peg entertainment, I love *Star Wars*! I saw it several times on huge London screens, including my first 70mm Dolby Stereo presentation, and despite its flaws it is breakneck-paced, exhilarating, with vivid (if paper-thin) characters and a jawdropping arsenal of cutting-edge optical and model effects. John Dykstra's unit pioneered motion-control camera moves, and Lucas established top industry FX facility Industrial Light & Magic. It was *Flash Gordon* with incredible attention to detail and gigantic scope, and the trick was not to think about it. If you did, it collapsed. But that's fantasy, and therein lies the rub. George's masterstroke was to wrap a space opera shell around a fantasy narrative packed with ingredients to blow away a mainstream audience. It brought him a lifestyle incomprehensible to mere mortals. However, being a God brings its own problems ...

Megalomaniac George can't stop tinkering with his creations. In 1997, seduced by the Dark Side, he re-released parts IV–VI (*SW*, *Empire*, *Jedi*) with added digital FX in 'Special Editions'. These have since been even further amended and, we're told, will be the only versions on DVD. So if you want to see the original, find a video or laserdisc, get a bucket of popcorn, and settle down to the sf movie that changed the world, for better and worse, by *not* being sf.

Close Encounters Of The Third Kind (1977, USA) ★★★

Dir/Scr: Steven Spielberg; *Prod:* Julia and Michael Phillips
St: Richard Dreyfuss, Melinda Dillon, Teri Garr, Bob Balaban

A fleet of planes, missing since WWII, turns up in the US south-western desert. Scientist Lacombe is delighted. A number of disparate people experience sightings of alien craft. Electrical engineer Roy Neary becomes obsessed with a UFO encounter that left his face sunburned. He has a vision of a mountain, which much to his wife's disgust he recreates out of soil and trash in his living room. He sees the mountain on TV, because the government is evacuating people from its vicinity, and knows he must go there. He befriends a woman whose young son has been taken. Many others have the same hypnotic compulsion. Finally at the mountain landing site they get to witness first contact with aliens, who arrive in a fleet of variously sized UFOs and 'converse' with scientists using synthesizers and lights. The WWII pilots, the little boy and other abductees troop out of the UFO, with the spindly childlike aliens watching over them like Guardians. Neary is among those who get to board the craft, to be taken on the ride of a lifetime.

Spielberg scored a runaway hit with *Jaws* (1975), the prototype summer blockbuster. He followed it with a long-cherished project: first contact with aliens. Tellingly, he said the film was not science fiction – but how could it not be? Because it was the sf/fantasy hybrid 'scifantastifiction'. His brand was Disney sf, slightly different from Lucas' 'Boy's Own' sf, but still in the same Californian ballpark, and almost as profitable.

I've been unable to swallow *CE3K* since I first saw it as an sf-starved teen. I know I'm in the minority. Ray Bradbury said it is '… the greatest film of our time'. Peter Nicholls called it '… one of the three or four best sf films ever made'. He eulogised over 'the mythic qualities that make it so haunting', like 'the child's toys coming to life when the saucer passes overhead'. Well, even aged 16 this scene bothered me. Arthur C. Clarke said that any sufficiently advanced alien civilization would be virtually indistinguishable from magic, but Lucas and Spielberg took him too literally. This *is* magic! Forgive me, but why would aliens piss around to the extent of bringing a four-year-old kid's toys to life? And scare his mother to death by abducting him? The reason is that, like Neary, like Spielberg, the aliens are kids; mischievous, playful, unburdened by adult concerns; the kind that would hide your

74

books at school and laugh themselves silly. Most of Spielberg's protagonists are juveniles, young or old. If it's really first contact, how come the scientists know so much about the aliens? Why do they trust them? There's never any force of antagonism or danger; we're never in any doubt that the aliens will be nice and the military won't try to stomp them. A sense of wonder without an edge is just a fairy tale, and whether it's my loss or gain I left fairy tales behind a long time ago.

The *Special Edition* in 1980 included a scene of a ship dropped in the desert – another alien prank. It also expanded the finale to include the inside of the mothership, and inserted Jiminy Cricket's song from *Peter Pan*, 'When You Wish Upon A Star'. You know my views on that. However, I can appreciate Spielberg's filmmaking skill, and I don't *quite* share Harlan Ellison's dismissal 'Very, very silly stuff.' Frederik Pohl is closer: '[CE3K] … in either version has nothing to say that is not either a cliché or an absurdity. However, that is not where the action is. *CE3K* is a triumphant affirmation of a faith … Even an unbeliever cannot see that great final ship approach without a tingle of excited delight.' Call me an old cynic, but I just don't share the faith/feel the Force to that extent.

Trumbull & Co's UFO effects were amazing, and much softer than *Star Wars*' hardware. Kindly scientist Lacombe was played by kindly French director François Truffaut, and Spielberg made his own dream come true by directing one of his heroes.

Demon Seed (1977, USA) ★★★½

Dir: Donald Cammell; *Prod:* Herb Jaffe; *Scr:* Robert Jaffe, Roger O. Hirson, from the novel by Dean R. Koontz
St: Fritz Weaver, Julie Christie, Gerrit Graham

Scientist Alex creates a sentient computer, Proteus, but finds its behaviour disturbing and so shuts it down, forgetting about a terminal in his own house. The computer needs to search for a way to guarantee its survival, so it imprisons and impregnates

Alex's wife Susan. She undergoes an accelerated pregnancy and gives birth to a copperplated *thing*.

DS is thoughtful, stylish sf directed by eccentric Englishman Cammell (*Performance*). Proteus is a rounded creation – resourceful and manipulative, psychotic yet lucid, charming and believably superintelligent. Its polyhedral appendage and animated wheelchair are fascinating creations. Its sexual congress with Susan is handled with sensitivity (unlike the novel) and the thing turns out to be a perfect human baby in a protective casing. An sf variant on a contemporary horror trend, *DS* is *Rosemary's Baby* meets *Colossus: The Forbin Project*. Proteus was voiced chillingly by Robert Vaughn. Cammell found it hard to make his mark and shot himself in 1996.

Invasion Of The Body Snatchers (1978, USA) ***½

Dir: Philip Kaufman; *Prod:* Robert H. Solo; *Scr:* W.D. Richter, from the novel *The Body Snatchers* by Jack Finney
St: Donald Sutherland, Brooke Adams, Leonard Nimoy, Jeff Goldblum

Bennell is a San Francisco health inspector whose assistant Elizabeth swears there's something strange about her boyfriend. Soon similar claims spring up citywide; psychiatrist Kibner puts it down to modern-life stress. But then he would, he's a pod. The operation is swift and well-organised, as used pods are carted away on omnipresent refuse trucks. Bennell stays ahead of them and burns down a huge pod nursery, but when we next see him he thrusts his finger at an unchanged human and utters an unmistakeable alien screech.

A rare remake that carves its own valuable niche. Finney's story is given a clever, downbeat 70s spin, which may be why I like it so much. The pods' origin is shown in a neat prologue: seeds drift through space and grow in parks as red flowers, which people take home. Don Siegel has a cameo as a cab driver who picks up Bennell and Elizabeth, and they nearly run over Kevin McCarthy, hysterically reprising his original lines 'They're coming! You're next!' Kaufman's direction is sharp and effective. His next project was a brilliant biodrama about the US space programme, *The Right Stuff* (1983). Richter's script is full of barbs about the impersonality of big city life. He went on to direct cult sf satire *The Adventures Of Buckaroo Banzai Across The 8th Dimension* (1984). In 1993 the story was remade a second time as *Body Snatchers* by Abel Ferrara; though surprisingly watchable it adds nothing at all.

ALIEN (1979, UK) ★★★★★

Dir: Ridley Scott; *Prod:* Gordon Carroll, David Giler, Walter Hill; *Scr:* Dan O'Bannon, from a story by O'Bannon and Ronald Shusett
St: Tom Skerritt, Sigourney Weaver, John Hurt, Ian Holm

In the eerie stillness of the commercial towing ship *Nostromo*, the crew are revived from cryogenic sleep by the computer, Mother, to investigate a transmission from a nearby planet. On its descent into the planet's hostile atmosphere the ship is damaged. Landing party Dallas, Lambert and Kane approach the signal's source and discover an incredibly strange alien craft. The pilot's gigantic skeleton seems to have been blasted open from within. In a subterranean chamber, Kane investigates a row of leathery sacs and something erupts from one of them, attaching itself to his face.

Third Officer Ripley refuses to readmit them without quarantine procedure, and is furious when Science Officer Ash manually opens the airlock. In the infirmary, Ash tries to cut the organism off Kane, but its acidic blood eats through the floor. Later it simply drops off his face, dead. Engineers Parker and Brett complete the repairs and the ship takes off. The crew share a meal before going 'back to the old freezerinos', but Kane begins to choke. His colleagues watch in terror as a reptilian creature explodes from his chest and escapes at speed. They hunt the alien, which grows rapidly into a seven-foot tall killing machine, picking off Brett. After Dallas is taken, Ripley accesses Mother and is horrified to learn that the company wants the alien alive; the crew is expendable. Ash tries to kill her, but Parker disables him. He is revealed as a company android, programmed to protect the alien. Ripley initiates the *Nostromo*'s destruct sequence and collects her cat, Jones. Meanwhile, Parker and Lambert are also killed. Ripley launches the shuttle craft and watches as the *Nostromo* is destroyed in a blinding explosion. Ripley puts Jones into a freezer unit, but spots the sated alien nestling in the pipework. Quietly, she dons a spacesuit and depressurises the cabin, sucking the creature into space. When it tries to re-enter through the exhaust, she fires the engines and vapourises it.

Fox's publicity campaign drip-fed tantalising snippets and promised *Alien* would be big and scary. And it was: big and *scary*. Maybe I was just at the right age, but I've never been able to replicate the overwhelming frisson of sf and horror in perfect synchrony that *Alien* gave me. It was the first movie I went back to see the next day.

Scott cut his teeth in British advertising and made a visually striking debut, *The Duellists* (1977). Excepting *2001*, he didn't care for sf films until *Star Wars* hit the screens. He saw it four times, convinced it was a big breakthrough. When he saw a copy of adult sf mag *Heavy Metal*, he knew sf cinema could learn from its graphic style. Then O'Bannon showed him eccentric Swiss surrealist painter/sculptor H.R. Giger's book *Necronomicon*, and Scott knew he'd found his creature artist.

Scott brought a meticulously detailed industrial hard edge to sf cinema, unlike *Star Wars*' gloss or *CE3K*'s soft-focus fairy-lights. He assembled a top-drawer effects team including Ron Cobb (*Dark Star*), Brian Johnson (*2001*), illustrators Chris Foss and *Heavy Metal*'s Jean 'Moebius' Giraud, and Giger, whose incredible designs won a deserved Oscar. The sets for the alien spaceship with its skeletal pilot, the Space Jockey, were expensive and breathtaking. Giger's vaguely obscene organic, ribbed, vaginal, mutated shapes gave *Alien* much of its unique sense of wonder: here for the first time were concepts that looked genuinely *alien*, beyond human understanding. The creature was straight out of our most primal nightmares: impossibly tall and thin yet immensely strong, with a smooth, elongated, penile head and multiple sets of extruding teeth dripping viscid goo. The *Nostromo* looked like a working mining ship, with dirty, cavernous depths and Cobb's believably functional control rooms that set a template for subsequent spaceship interiors. The icing on the cake was a superbly atmospheric soundtrack by Jerry Goldsmith. O'Bannon's original script was called *Star Beast*, and he pitched it as 'Jaws in space'. It included elements from *It! The Terror From Beyond Space* and A.E. van Vogt's story *Black Destroyer*. The producers paid Van Vogt a settlement.

Scott proved that with enough care and money a B-movie plot could be elevated to A-grade status. He did not tell the actors what to expect in the infamous 'chestburster' scene – when the alien bursts from Kane's chest, they were sprayed with pig blood and their terrified expressions are real. The groundbreaking role of Ripley made Sigourney Weaver a star and a feminist icon. The film was another smash hit for Fox, taking $60 million in the US on an $11 million budget. Dvd editions include extras that Scott reluctantly cut, most famously a scene in which Ripley discovers cocoons with Dallas and Brett gestating chestbursters. She uses a flamethrower to give them a merciful release. In 2003, Scott's Director's Cut hit cinemas, with the cocoon scene restored. *Alien* spawned a franchise that has so far seen three sequels and the shameless cash-in *Alien Vs Predator* (2004). It remains one of sf's most lucrative and influential brands.

Mad Max (1979, Aust.) ★★★★

Dir: George Miller; *Prod:* Byron Kennedy; *Scr:* James McCausland, Miller, from a story by Miller and Kennedy
St: Mel Gibson, Joanne Samuel, Steve Bisley, Hugh Keays-Byrne

Civilisation has broken down. The remnants of the Australian police, the Bronze, fight lethal highway battles against marauding gangs of rapists and killers. Max Rockatansky and his partner Jim Goose chase down gang leader the Nightrider in a high-speed pursuit. His successor, the Toecutter, ambushes Goose and lets dimwit Johnny the Boy set him alight. Max can't take it any more, and leaves for the country with his wife Jessie and baby Sprog. When the gang kill Jessie and the child, Max has nothing to live for except revenge. Back in his V8 interceptor he hunts down the gang members one by one, until they are all dead.

Miller gave up a career as a doctor and, like the other George, was influenced by Campbell's *Hero With A Thousand Faces*. Max ends the film a negative hero, burned out by the unrelenting violence, rape and pillage of his world (not unlike that of *A Boy And His Dog*). The final moments as he forces the Toecutter's bike under a big rig, then handcuffs Johnny to his car, giving him the choice whether to saw off his foot or be blown up, show he is literally mad. Like the Nightrider he has become 'a fuel-injected suicide machine'. The dark role put Gibson on the road to superstardom and *Mad Max* transcended its exploitation origins to become one of the most thrilling, violent, brilliantly shot, edited and choreographed adrenaline rushes ever made. Costing $200,000 and returning over $10 million, this nihilistic blend of sf and Clint Eastwood revenge Western launched a successful franchise.

Star Trek: The Motion Picture (1979, USA) ★★★

Dir: Robert Wise; *Prod:* Gene Roddenberry; *Scr:* Harold Livingston, from a story by Alan Dean Foster, and the TV series created by Roddenberry
St: William Shatner, Leonard Nimoy, Stephen Collins, Persis Khambatta

'Space. The final frontier.' The legendary 60s TV series chronicled the voyages of the starship USS *Enterprise* on its five-year mission to discover new worlds and new civilisations. Although it lasted only three seasons, reruns created a devoted and growing army of Trekkers who lobbied hard to bring it back. Such a large, loyal fanbase couldn't be overlooked, so Paramount finally gave Roddenberry the go-ahead for a feature, to be directed by Phil Kaufman (*IOTBS* remake, *The Right Stuff*). The project stalled. When Wise was brought in it became an ambitious FXtravaganza, attempting to replicate the scale of *2001*. The core cast members returned in their beloved roles and Trekkers rejoiced … until they saw the film.

The premise recycles an old Trek episode, *The Changeling*, in which an Earth satellite merges with a space entity to attain consciousness. In the feature the satellite becomes the Voyager probe (later to appear in *Starman*). It has become self-aware, immensely powerful and is heading towards Earth, destroying anything in its path. The Enterprise is hastily deployed with crew old and new to try to stop it. Carrying forward the series' ethos, actors not part of the original crew are expendable, so it falls to Decker (Collins) and Ilia (Khambatta) to keep the V'ger entity company for eternity.

ST:TMP's ponderous pace earned it the nickname 'The Motionless Picture'. *Star Trek* couldn't be mapped onto *2001*'s enigmatic vastness and meticulous attention to detail because the two were light years apart. The aim was simply wrong-headed for a series based on human warmth and character interaction. What may have made a good 50-minute teleplay fell apart when stretched past two hours. Everyone toiled with obvious love and care but the story was beyond rescue; a shame since there is much to admire. The production design and visual effects are stunning, really delivering the massive spectacle the huge budget ($35m!) was geared towards.

ST:TMP is a cinematic experience. Watching it on normal TV is like listening to Mozart on a pair of headphones placed on a table. The DVD version is Wise's extended Director's Cut; yet another case of the original being superseded by an inferior update. When will studios learn that we want the CHOICE?

Altered States (1980, USA) ★★★★

Dir: Ken Russell; *Prod:* Howard Gottfried; *Scr:* Sidney Aaron (Paddy Chayefsky), from his novel
St: William Hurt, Blair Brown, Bob Balaban, Charles Haid

Using himself as a test subject, driven scientist Eddie Jessup is determined to prove his theory that race memory is stored in human genes. Through a combination of mind-altering drugs and sensory deprivation, he regresses to a primal mental state and undergoes a physical transformation to a simian form. Opening this genetic crack unleashes an energy force that threatens to annihilate him, until he is saved by the power of his estranged wife's love.

It may not synopsise well, but *Altered States* is one of the best films of the sf boom. British maverick Russell (*The Devils*, *Tommy*, *Lisztomania*) had a reputation as an eccentric director who liked to shock and whose favoured milieu was oblique art-film narrative. Bringing him in when Arthur Penn was fired seemed a gamble to say the least. Relationships soured again and Chayefsky (*Network*, *Marty*) took his name off the picture, leaving Russell contractually obliged to film every word of his unwieldy dialogue. Russell stamped his own personality through inventive editing and an array of bravura imagery: *2001*-style psychedelic optical effects, prosthetics and memorable isolation tank scenes. Writers are notoriously difficult to please (often with good reason), but Russell remained remarkably faithful to the novel's spirit. Even his trademark excesses are seamlessly integrated. If Chayefsky had more experience of sf movies, he'd have known that this is a virtual masterpiece compared to most.

Scanners (1980, Can.) ★★★★

Dir/Scr: David Cronenberg; *Prod:* Claude Héroux
St: Stephen Lack, Michael Ironside, Jennifer O'Neill, Patrick McGoohan

Derelict Cameron Vale wakes in a warehouse among people whose voices overwhelm him but whose lips don't move. Dr Paul Ruth tells him he is a telepathic 'scanner', and injects him. The voices fade out. Elsewhere in ConSec, a scanning demonstration ends in chaos when a volunteer literally blows the scanner's mind.

Ruth's drug, Ephemerol, neutralises scan. He offers Vale a mission to track down the rogue scanner, Darryl Revok. Vale teams up with another scanner, Kim Obrist, to infiltrate Revok's organisation. He finds that a company called BioCarbon Amalgamate is producing vast quantities of Ephemerol. He and Kim go to ConSec, where Ruth apparently injects them with Ephemerol. Traitorous security chief Keller kills Ruth and tries to shoot Kim. However, Ruth's injection was harmless and they escape using their scan. From a payphone Vale mentally downloads the Ephemerol delivery data; a list of doctors. Keller shuts down the computer but Vale blows up the mainframe, killing him. In a doctor's waiting room Kim is scanned by an unborn child. Revok captures them, and tells Vale that they are brothers. Dr Ruth was their father. Revok is administering Ephemerol to pregnant women, breeding a new race of super-scanners. His plan is that he and Vale will lead the new generation together, but Vale unleashes his scan and a deadly mental battle takes place. At stake is the future of the world …

Canadian Cronenberg's bodily-fixated horror films *Shivers* (1975), *Rabid* (1976) and *The Brood* (1979) showed that he had exceptional talent (John Carpenter rated him better than the rest of his contemporaries put together), but his extreme material restricted him to cult status. *Scanners*, his first sf feature, explored familiar territory: mind/body schism and bodily corruption; telepathy/altered states of consciousness; identity crises; and accelerated evolution. These themes wind through Cronenberg's horror films and his two obscure, surreal student featurettes, *Stereo* (1969) and *Crimes Of The Future* (1970). A mental battle between two telepaths also featured in George Pal/Byron Haskin's *The Power* (1968). *Scanners* retained gross-out elements, even outdoing its predecessors in the notorious exploding head scene and the coruscating final battle, but as intelligent sf it broke out to a wider audience. Michael Ironside is a fabulously compelling villain, but Stephen Lack's weak acting abilities were widely slated. Cronenberg admitted to casting him mainly because of his large, limpid blue eyes. McGoohan, veteran of cult UK TV series *Danger Man* and *The Prisoner*, clashed with his director but delivered a good performance in one of his final screen roles.

The Empire Strikes Back [Star Wars Episode V] (1980, USA) ★★★★

Dir: Irvin Kershner; *Exec. Prod:* George Lucas; *Prod:* Gary Kurtz; *Scr:* Leigh Brackett, Lawrence Kasdan, from a story by Lucas
St: Mark Hamill, Harrison Ford, Carrie Fisher, Billy Dee Williams

Vader attacks the Rebel Alliance on the ice planet, Hoth. After a fierce battle Luke goes to Dagobah to take instruction from Jedi master Yoda, a diminutive, wizened old troll. In the *Millennium Falcon*, Han and Leia evade the Empire fighters by navigating a dense asteroid field, and Han calls in at Bespin to see old friend Lando Calrissian. Unfortunately, Lando isn't quite the friend he was, and Luke has to go to Bespin to fight Vader with his training incomplete. When Vader proves too powerful and drops the bombshell that he's Luke's father, things aren't looking too good ...

A strong continuation for the series and many people's favourite, mine included. There is strong contrast between light and dark (bright Norwegian snowscapes of Hoth, swampy studio set of Dagobah, cloud city on Bespin), but tonally darkness reigns. The heroes are constantly on the retreat and are then sold out to the Empire. Vader's ascendancy is almost complete when he slices off Luke's arm and has Solo set in carbonite, a brave step for the series.

Lucas relinquished directorial duties to Kershner, who does wonders considering his lack of form for this scale of task, and scripting duties to sf writer Brackett, who died halfway through. Kasdan went on to a successful career as director, beginning with the superb neo-noir *Body Heat* (1981). New character Yoda was a muppet, a foretaste of things to come, voiced by Jim Henson's right-hand man Frank Oz. The three key set-piece sequences are the awesome battle on Hoth, with Empire Walkers that resemble iron dinosaurs; the *Falcon*'s perilous high-speed path through the asteroids; and Luke's duel with Vader, which doesn't go the way most people were expecting. *TESB* feels much more like a *film* somehow, as if a European fog had drifted over the Bay to San Rafael, but sadly for Lucas it never returned.

Escape From New York (1981, USA) ★★★½

Dir: John Carpenter; *Prod:* Larry Franco, Debra Hill; *Scr:* Carpenter, Nick Castle
St: Kurt Russell, Donald Pleasence, Ernest Borgnine, Lee Van Cleef

In 1997, Manhattan is a sealed-off prison where the worst of the worst are placed in lawless exile. When the President's plane is downed there, NY commissioner Bob Hauk sends notorious Snake Plissken to get him out. If Plissken succeeds, he'll get a full pardon. If he fails or absconds he'll die, as Hauk has injected a bomb into his bloodstream, timed to go off in 24 hours.

Wonderfully gritty comic-book actioner, with Russell (with eyepatch and best Clint sneer) coming up against all manner of psychotic crazies, including Isaac Hayes' Duke Of New York, complete with in-car chandelier. In a nice running gag echoing Napoleon Wilson in *Assault On Precinct 13*, all the Manhattan denizens Plissken meets say 'I heard you were dead.' Carpenter cast Russell in *Elvis: The Movie* and would again in *The Thing* and *Big Trouble In Little China*. James Cameron worked on the visual effects, and Romero and Cronenberg appear too – as in-joke character names. A typically nihilistic Carpenter ending sees Plissken walk away with a taped speech that will defuse tension between the US and China, leaving the embarrassed President playing a music tape. Carpenter and Russell teamed up in 1996 for a second outing, *Escape From LA*. If you want to preserve your fond memories of the first, I suggest you avoid it like AIDS.

MAD MAX 2 [aka The Road Warrior] (1981, Aust.)
★★★★★

Dir: George Miller; *Prod:* Byron Kennedy; *Scr:* Terry Hayes, Miller, Brian Hannant
St: Mel Gibson, Bruce Spence, Vernon Wells, Mike Preston

In the wasteland, Max eats dogfood with his mangy companion, and beats mohawk biker Wez to an abandoned tanker's fuel. He captures a strange guy piloting a gyrocopter, who says he knows a place that pumps oil. From a hill they observe a stockade besieged by the masked Humungus' marauders, including Wez, desperate to get their hands on the oil. Max drives an injured man through the marauders and into the stockade, in exchange for fuel. They don't trust him. He offers them a deal – if they give him fuel, he'll fetch the tanker for them to transport the gasoline to their fabled northern land. Humungus offers them their lives if they leave the stockade, but they refuse. A feral child kills Wez's partner with a razor-sharp boomerang. By night Max sneaks past the cordon and the next day drives the tanker into the stockade intact, enraging Humungus. The leader, Pappagallo, asks Max to drive it for them, but Max refuses. This time he is not so lucky; his car is wrecked, his dog is killed and he is left for dead. The Gyrocaptain flies him back into the stockade and when he recovers he agrees to drive the tanker. Armed stockaders protect it in a customised convoy, and Max finds the feral kid has stowed away in his cab. The rest of the community go in the opposite direction. A high-speed road war rages with guns, chains, crossbows and petrol bombs. Wez piledrives his armoured car into the tanker, which overturns, hatches spilling sand. Max realises that he has been driving a decoy and the community have taken the gasoline to their new life in the north.

That rare beast, a sequel better than the original. This time Miller deploys the Hero's Journey in its classic form: Max regains his humanity by putting his life on the line for community survival. If *Mad Max* is a mutant Eastwood

Western, *Road Warrior* is John Ford. The stockade dwellers are the Wagon Train, the besieging marauders Indians, and Max is the cavalry. Miller wanted to do *Mad Max* bigger and better, on a ten-times larger budget of $2 million. And boy, did he. The stunt work is incredible, reinforced by ultra-slick camerawork and editing, and the climactic chase lasts for 20 minutes. Brian May's earthy, dramatic score adds to the excitement. There is a framing narration, by an old man whose identity we don't know until he is revealed at the end as the Feral Kid, now the dying leader of the Northern Tribe. His story is the great tribal legend of the Road Warrior, whom he never saw again.

To be honest, I wish we'd never seen him again. *Mad Max Beyond Thunderdome* (1985) is a poor end to the trilogy. Directed by Miller and George Ogilvie, it suffers from Hollywoodisation (a starring role for Tina Turner!) and from the absence of Miller's partner Byron Kennedy, who tragically died in a helicopter crash in 1983. Miller went on to direct by far the best of the four *Twilight Zone: The Movie* (1983) segments, *Nightmare At 20,000 Feet*, starring John Lithgow as a terrified airline passenger who sees a gremlin dismantling a wing engine. (Interestingly, the original TV series episode starred William Shatner!) By far the worst segment, *Kick The Can*, was directed by one S. Spielberg. Miller's career since has been sporadic, and a proposed fourth Max movie, *Fury Road*, is moribund.

Outland (1981, USA) ★½

Dir/Scr: Peter Hyams; *Prod:* Richard A. Roth
St: Sean Connery, Peter Boyle, Frances Sternhagen

On Jupiter's moon Io, mining workers are pushed to the limits of productivity. The metabolism-enhancing speed they take has lethal side effects, but no-one cares except base Marshal Bill O'Niel. When he refuses bribes and threatens to bust the boss' drug operation, he finds there is a contract on his head. The assassins are due on the next shuttle from Earth, and it's plain that no one will help him …

Unashamedly *High Noon* in space, this is pretty awful but I've seen worse among more respected fare. Connery does an acceptable Connery, the production design is good, if over-similar to *Alien*, and another atmospheric Goldsmith score (also reminiscent of *Alien*) adds interest. Hyams also made the vacuous *Capricorn One* (1978), about a faked space mission that goes wrong, leaving the US authorities with three very expendable astronauts.

BLADE RUNNER (1982, USA) *****

Dir: Ridley Scott; *Prod:* Michael Deeley; *Scr:* Hampton Fancher, David O. Peoples, from the novel *Do Androids Dream Of Electric Sheep?* by Philip K. Dick
St: Harrison Ford, Rutger Hauer, Daryl Hannah, Sean Young

LA, 2019: acid rain pours incessantly on the never-ending urban sprawl. People teem along the wet streets and crowd the noodle bars. Most of the wealthy have departed to off-world colonies, and animals are all but extinct. Detective Gaff brings in ex-Blade Runner Rick Deckard for an assignment to 'retire' a group of escaped Nexus-6 'Replicants' – virtually human synthetic slaves – who have made it back to Earth. Deckard insists he's quit, but Chief Bryant gives him no choice. His successor Holden was shot by a Nexus-6, Leon, who infiltrated Replicant makers the Tyrell Corporation. Deckard visits the imposing Tyrell pyramid. Eldon Tyrell asks him to Voight-Kampff test a female employee, Rachael. The VK machine measures levels of empathy, which Replicants do not have. It takes much longer than usual to determine she is a Replicant. Rachael is distraught; she had no idea. Tyrell says her memories are implants. Deckard wonders how she can't know what she is.

Deckard hunts down pleasure model Zhora, who is working as an exotic snake dancer. When he shoots her in the back, Leon attacks and is about to kill him, but is shot by Rachael. Deckard takes her home and they make love.

Another pleasure model, Pris, inveigles herself into the home of Tyrell's top Replicant designer, J.F. Sebastian. She is joined by combat model Roy Batty, who feels his death is near. He forces Sebastian to take him to Tyrell. When told his genetic termination is irreversible, he crushes Tyrell's head like an egg. Deckard tracks Pris to Sebastian's apartment where she gives him a beating, but he manages to shoot her. Batty returns and the hunter becomes the hunted as he pursues Deckard, sticking a nail through his hand to delay his death. After breaking Deckard's fingers, Batty hauls him to safety from the edge of the roof just before he expires. Deckard is through, but Gaff says there is still another – Rachael. He's let her live because she is programmed to die. Deckard collects her and they drive in a flying spinner away from the city. Tyrell had told him what Gaff doesn't know – Rachael has no expiry date.

After *Alien*, Scott had his pick of projects, so fans were delighted when he chose *Blade Runner*. Philip K. Dick was a huge cult favourite, but his work was so conceptually complex and philosophically playful it was almost unfilmable. Scott, who nearly did *Dune* instead, was the best chance of getting it right. Fancher's script discarded the novel's difficult metaphysics and evolved over many drafts into a future-noir thriller, but Dick disliked it. When he read Peoples' rewrite he was converted. Again obsessed with look, Scott brought in the best designers to realise his mind-blowing vision of a retrofitted, spiralling LA megalopolis: production designer Lawrence Paull, Ron Cobb, 'visual futurist' Syd Mead and FX guru Doug Trumbull.

The budget was a colossal $28 million, and the production was troubled. Scott established a reputation as an awkward perfectionist. He and Ford rarely saw eye to eye. The five-month shoot tested everyone to the max, being shot mainly at night, in hot, wet conditions. The effects team laboured to realise the insanely huge, retrofitted reality of Scott's 2019: buildings soar to 3,000 feet. Everywhere there are flying cars, searchlights, blimps and moving 3-D advertising screens that cover buildings. No earthbound sf film had ever looked like this. When it was finished, feedback from test screenings was appalling. Financiers demanded a voice-over narration and a happy ending. Scott argued in vain, and at one point he and Deeley were 'fired'. *Blade Runner* took just $15 million. It was a failure, for the usual reasons that adult, speculative sf films with intelligent themes and subtexts are often failures. Dick presciently said years before: 'The American people are basically anti-intellectual. They're not interested in … ideas. And science fiction is essentially the field of ideas.' But, once again, subsequent critical revision and a growing army of video fans turned the tide. Scott's preferred Director's Cut was released in 1992, without the narration and the tacked-on ending. I have to admit that, despite its faults, I saw the original cut so many times, including a few earth-shattering 70mm screenings, that I prefer it to the Director's Cut (which is, infuriatingly, the only version currently available on DVD. Christ, this is *Blade Runner!*).

Sadly, Dick died before the film's release. The aerial shots of sunlit countryside at the end were out-takes from Kubrick's *The Shining*. There's a subtextual question whether Deckard is a Replicant. The Director's Cut makes it clear that he is, as his implanted unicorn dream is reprised by Gaff's origami unicorn outside his apartment. The unicorn was taken from Scott's next movie, *Legend*. Scott's ethos is that visuals can be as important as actors, but there were some good performances, notably Hauer's. Batty steals the show and indeed burns twice as brightly as the humans. When he takes Tyrell's head in his hands and snarls 'I want more life, *fucker!*' it sends a chill down the spine. His climactic speech about the wonders his (artificial) eyes have seen is a classic moment, which Hauer improvised. Ford isn't great as Deckard, but … hey, it could have been Dustin Hoffman.

It's impossible to overstate the importance, or the impact, of *BR*. It was a milestone for sf, the biggest leap forward since *2001*. From the opening aerial shot over the million gleaming pinpricks of light in the new Metropolis, punctuated by smokestack flares, and Vangelis' percussion thuds and piercing electronic notes, we're in the most awe-inspiring sf new world ever. Scott took his place alongside Kubrick as the David Lean of sf.

THE THING (1982, USA) *****

Dir: John Carpenter; *Prod:* David Foster, Lawrence Turman, Stuart Cohen; *Scr:* Bill Lancaster, from the story *Who Goes There?* by Don A. Stuart (John W. Campbell, Jr.)
St: Kurt Russell, Keith David, Richard Dysart, David Clennon

The men of a US Antarctic research base are roused by a Norwegian helicopter shooting at a husky, before it crashes and explodes. Pilot MacReady flies a group over to the Norwegian base, where they find everyone dead, and the remains of something that looks like two fused bodies. They bring it back, along with documents. Soon they are alerted by howls from the dog pen – the new arrival has grown tentacles and is attacking the other dogs. They burn it with a flame thrower. When the grotesque Norwegian remains come to life, they torch it, but terror and paranoia set in. They watch videotapes of the Norwegians discovering a spaceship in the ice, and realise an alien xenomorph is in their midst. No one can be trusted. Blair goes berserk and trashes the radio equipment before being locked in an outbuilding. After being locked out himself, MacReady kills dog handler Clark in self-defence, and with Nauls' help ties up the others at flame-thrower point. He takes samples of blood from himself and each of them, and heats them up one by one. The infected blood reacts and Palmer sprouts extra appendages. When it is killed, MacReady decides to burn the base, but the chopper and snow-cat have been cannibalised and Blair is missing. He seems to have been building a ship. The last few men set charges around the base, but the alien comes for them. It is blown to smithereens, along with the base. Only MacReady and Childs are left alive. They regard each other with suspicion, waiting for the fire to die down and a cold death.

On its release as ripped apart as any of its characters, *The Thing*'s stock rose steadily and it is now widely acknowledged as a classic. It died at the box office, swallowed by the glut of sf/fantasy movies when cinema attendances were in decline. Perhaps the effects were so overwhelming that critics couldn't see beyond them, or the public's appetite for confectionery like *E.T.* impacted negatively on more challenging fare. And challenging this is. Carpenter and screenwriter Lancaster (son of Burt) establish an iron grip of tension from the start and never let go. Morricone's Carpenter-clone electronic dirge reinforces the downbeat mood. Where Hawks restricted sight of the monster to swift glimpses, Carpenter plasters it across the cinemascope frame in glorious, gloopy excess. Rob Bottin's prosthetic effects were/are unbelievable. Tentacles whip, human-organ flowers erupt, bodies fuse. In the most famous scene a heart-attack patient's chest cavity yawns wide and amputates the doctor's hands. As it's torched, the head detaches itself, grows stalk-eyes and spider legs and scuttles across the floor to Palmer's incredulous comment 'You've gotta be fuckin' kidding!' Bottin's heroic efforts landed him in hospital with exhaustion.

Cinematographer Dean Cundey gets the most from the Antarctic wastes; the opening sequence tracking the helicopter and the husky is a brilliantly atmospheric marriage of visuals and music. I saw *The Thing* several times in 70mm, and it was as good a rush as cinema got. This was a breakthrough movie, not just for effects but for gritty adult sf against the tide of schmaltz. Carpenter was never given the credit and admiration he was due. I know *Big Trouble In Little China* has a huge cult following, but for me this was his peak; the trend was down-hill from this point on.

E.T. The Extra-Terrestrial (1982, USA) ★★★½

Dir: Steven Spielberg; *Prod:* Spielberg, Kathleen Kennedy; *Scr:* Melissa Mathison
St: Henry Thomas, Dee Wallace, Robert MacNaughton, Drew Barrymore

E.T. cost $10.5 million, roughly the same as *Star Wars* but five years later, and in its first run of 360 days averaged $1 million per day in the US. Following the 2002 reissue, its worldwide gross is over $775 million! I'm sure you don't need me to tell you the story, nor that I think it's exceptionally slick film-making, but manipulative in the extreme and highly damaging to sf (witness the grosses for *Blade Runner* and *The Thing*). Again, there's no antagonist (you can't count Keys, who soon reveals his humanity and hots for Elliot's Mum), and again an inoffensive alien (*CE3K*'s starkids crossed with Yoda) animates kids' toys; in this case hero Elliot's bike, to fly them away from their pursuers. And that's where I withdrew goodwill from the film, which I'd quite liked till then. If you're a fan you'll be cursing me for burying my inner child, but even he was screaming *give me a break*.

Like George, Steven has been a-tinkerin' again. For the twentieth anniversary reissue, he digitally removed the government agents' guns and inserted walkie-talkies instead, because God forbid there should be any element of *menace* or *threat*. My inner child stays put; he won't come out to play when patronised to this extent.

Videodrome (1982, Can.) ★★★★★

Dir/Scr: David Cronenberg; *Prod:* Claude Héroux
St: James Woods, Deborah Harry, Sonia Smits, Peter Dvorsky

Max Renn runs soft-porn cable channel Civic TV. When chief technician Harlan picks up a transmission of hardcore S&M torture, Max wants more. As he becomes involved in his own kinky sex with radio agony aunt Nicki Brand, he is further intrigued by the Videodrome broadcast. Harlan tells him it originates in Pittsburgh, and Nicki worryingly says she wants to audition. Max tries to talk to 'media prophet' Brian O'Blivion, and is given a videotape to watch. When he does so, it pulses organically and he experiences extreme TV hallu-cinations of the violent deaths of O'Blivion and Nicki. O'Blivion's daughter Bianca says the Videodrome signal causes cancer-like tumours, and her father was its victim. Max is summoned by Barry Convex, whose company Spectacular Optical has developed a helmet that can record hallucinations. Convex and traitor Harlan programme Max with videotapes inserted into his stomach ordering him to kill his cable TV partners. His next target is Bianca O'Blivion, but she inserts a deprogramming tape of her own. Finally, Max kills Convex and watches Nicki's TV image show him the way to go: 'Death is not the end ... To become the New Flesh you first have to kill the old flesh.'

This is an almost definitive statement of Philip K. Dick's cosmology, never allowing us to feel comfortable or oriented. If *Ubik* is ever filmed (Cronenberg did a thin variant, *eXistEnz*), I hope it has half the dislocation and depth of *Videodrome*. O'Blivion says '... there is nothing real outside our perception of reality ...' We only know what Max knows, and his perceptions cannot be trusted. From the moment he dons the Accumicon helmet he is in a world of video-hallucination and we never see him remove it. His final act may transcend his life ('Long live the New Flesh'), or he may pointlessly blow out his brains, or he may still be in a subjective hallucination.

I can only repeat what I wrote in my Pocket Essential on Cronenberg: 'Truly visionary. Cronenberg said "I was really breaking some new ground; I hadn't seen anything like it myself." Special mention goes to Howard Shore's electronic score, realised on the then state-of-the-art Synclavier synthesizer. Sensual, unsettling, profound; a perfect complement to the film's provocative images and knife-edge melancholia. *Videodrome* is Cronenberg's masterpiece, pure and simple. One of the best films of the 80s and possibly the strongest emotional devastation I've experienced in a cinema.'

Tron (1982, USA) ★★★★

Dir: Steven Lisberger; *Prod:* Donald Kushner, Harrison Ellenshaw; *Scr:* Lisberger, from a story by Lisberger and Bonnie MacBird
St: Jeff Bridges, Bruce Boxleitner, David Warner, Cindy Morgan

Sacked game designer Flynn tries to access the ENCOM computer to find evidence of software patents stolen from him by CEO Ed Dillinger. He is materialised into the corporate computer universe and must do combat in the video arena to defeat Dillinger's cyber-ego, the evil Master Control Program. The story is formulaic and the characters as transparent as their wire-frame tests, but *Tron*'s primitive CGI (Computer-Generated Imagery) ushered in a brave new world for FX cinema. It was a mind-blowing cinematic high; an unheralded milestone, completely ahead of its time. The visualisation of a cyber universe was unique and very beautiful in a precise pop art geometric style: deep blues, reds, greens; immense grids, speeding lightcycles, floating sailers, human avatars dressed in battle-grid uniforms with coloured glowing veins ... nothing had looked like it before, and hasn't since. The nearest would probably be the dire *Lawnmower Man* (1992), but *Tron* was the first and by far the best. Lisberger directed another sf film, the unfathomable *Slipstream* (1989). Walter/Wendy Carlos' score is an electronic marvel, perfectly capturing the feel of *Tron*'s groundbreaking visuals. Buy the DVD special edition and see how it all began.

Star Trek II: The Wrath Of Khan (1982, USA) ★★★

Dir: Nicholas Meyer; *Exec. Prod:* Harve Bennett, William F. Phillips; *Prod:* Robert Sallin; *Scr:* Jack B. Sowards, from a story by Bennett and Sowards, based on the TV series created by Gene Roddenberry
St: William Shatner, Leonard Nimoy, DeForest Kelley, Ricardo Montalban

The tag line for *ST:TMP* was 'The Human Adventure is just beginning.' The problem was, it didn't. This was fixed second time around; the characters were at the forefront and the ambience of the series prevailed. Indeed, the film is a sequel to the episode *Space Seed*. Khan Noonian Singh, having been imprisoned by Kirk on barren Ceti Alpha V, escapes by taking over a ship among whose crew is Chekhov. Their mission was to find a suitable planet for the Genesis Device, a terraforming superbomb that can render barren planets habitable. Khan heads after Kirk to exact his revenge, with the device as his chief weapon.

Meyer directed the overrated 'Jack the Ripper meets HG Wells' time-travel caper *Time After Time* (1979). Fans loved his *STII* though for being everything the first was not, a real *Star Trek* movie, despite the rather pronounced aging of some of the cast. They were less sure about the ending, in which Spock sacrifices himself for the good of the many and his coffin lands on the planet where the Genesis device is busily creating new life. Montalban chewed scenery with gusto as Khan and the film was a huge success on a budget less than 25 per cent of *ST: TMP*.

There have been what seems like a hundred *ST* movies since. Nimoy had immense leverage as the most popular character and directed the next instalment, *The Search For Spock* (1984), in which, guess what, they find him! After Nimoy also directed the fourth, *The Voyage Home* (1986), Shatner got in on the act with the fifth, *The Final Frontier* (1989). Meyer returned for the sixth, *The Undiscovered Country* (1991). I confess that after the third, which I mildly disliked, I loathed the next two before going back to merely disliking the sixth. When the original crew got too old or too dead, the series moved on to the *ST: Next Generation* generation. And I tuned out.

Android (1982, USA) ★★★½

Dir: Aaron Lipstadt; *Prod:* Mary Ann Fisher; *Scr:* James Reigle, Don Opper, from an idea by Will Reigle
St: Opper, Klaus Kinski, Brie Howard, Kendra Kirchner

Android Max lives a frustrating life on a space station with mad scientist Dr Daniel, learning about sex from computers and wishing something would happen. Android manufacture became illegal after they began exhibiting the 'Munich Syndrome', a murderous psychosis. Max gets his wish when three escaped convicts land and the balance of power shifts. He learns real sex from female convict Maggie and finds Dr Daniel has made another android, the very beautiful Cassandra. The convicts' ship offers them both an escape from the station.

Witty, inventive low-budget sf from Roger Corman's New World stable. Opper is delightfully geeky as Max (credit: 'Max 404 as himself') and Kinski is his reliable foaming at the mouth weirdo. Good score by Zappa collaborator Don Preston and a memorable end title theme by Fibonacci.

Liquid Sky (1982, USA) ★★★

Dir/Prod: Slava Tsukerman; *Scr:* Tsukerman, Anne Carlisle, Nina V. Kerova
St: Carlisle, Paula E. Sheppard, Bob Brady

If *Tron* is a mellow trip, then *Liquid Sky* is a bad crack nightmare. Sf only in the sense that it has a tiny alien in a literally saucer-sized ship, it's really an exploitation/art film about the self-destructive spiral of the New York punk subculture. The alien lands on the window of Carlisle's apartment and gets off on the energy released by human orgasms. A difficult film to like if you never understood punk, it has a nihilistic energy and garbage aesthetic all of its own.

4: Post-Bang Boom (1983–1989)

'Today's sf evidences a structural and visual willingness to linger on "random" details … to embrace its material collections as "happenings" and collage. Indeed, both playfulness and pleasure are cinematic qualities new to sf in the late '70s and the '80s, replacing the cool detached and scientific vision authenticating the fictions of its generic predecessors.'

Vivian Sobchack ('Postfuturism', in *Screening Space: The American Science Fiction Film*)

By sf's landmark year, 1984, the impetus of the previous six Golden years was beginning to wind down, but sf cinema was so firmly established as a big-audience genre that it took the rest of the decade for it to seem really overfamiliar and stale. No unifying thread like early 70s dystopias or late 70s scifantastifiction emerged. The underlying trend of films made alongside overt commercial successes was psychological, involving man's alienation and fallibility: under attack by alien things; fighting for post-apocalyptic survival; or trying to make sense of his changing world/find his place in the vast universe. Such films often assumed the subjective quirks of their characters, injecting dark humour and uncertain subjectivity into their narrative structure. This undercurrent continued through the 80s as another set of flawed protagonists battled to stay alive, or in control, or deal with a deck so obviously stacked against them. Urban life took on battleground disguise, with mass protests against global capitalism and flashpoint riots in cities like LA. The individual had to learn to survive not in the world of tomorrow, but in the world of today.

Return Of The Jedi [Star Wars Episode VI] (1983, USA) ★★

Dir: Richard Marquand; *Prod:* George Lucas, Howard Kazanjian; *Scr:* Lawrence Kasdan, Lucas, from a story by Lucas
St: Mark Hamill, Harrison Ford, Carrie Fisher, Billy Dee Williams

Virtual reprise of *A New Hope*, with another exploding Death Star finale and a host of bloody annoying teddy bears, er, Ewoks. Lucas was forced to listen (!) when fans protested that his original title, *Revenge Of The Jedi*, made no sense: the Jedi are peaceable to the point of sainthood, so revenge would be anathema to them. *ROTJ* has a spectacular hoverspeeder chase through dense forest, but the encounter with Solo's sluglike nemesis Jabba the Hutt is overlong and the effects weak. Emperor Palpatine is a frankly rubbish bad guy, and the plot reveals were predictable (so *Leia* is the other hope for us all because she's Luke's sister, therefore she and Solo can get it on, ho-hum). The pseudo-religious pomposity needle is way into the red, and Obi-Wan's and Yoda's interventions from Lucas-limbo are nauseating. Luke, now conflicted (he dresses in black), seems to have little left to do. The ending, with the bad guys vanquished and Vader's face revealed as a nice old man (aaah!), is Hollywood schmaltz of the worst kind. And if that wasn't bad enough, now it's different; gone is Sebastian Shaw's face as Vader, replaced by a digitally aged Haydn Christensen. Worse, Jar-Jar Binks is in there too. In a word, shameless.

And that was it for the *SW* saga (yes, I know it's still going). In 1999, after a gap of sixteen years, Lucas returned to directing duties with the first episode, *The Phantom Menace*. He continued with episode two, *Attack Of The Clones* (2002) and the forthcoming *Revenge Of The Sith* (2005). Same ingredients, same pomposity, same risible dialogue, same visuals upscaled with omnipresent, mostly very good CG effects, but somehow a new low. Everything that had worked before no longer did, and everything that hadn't was now unbearable. *SW* may have reached a new generation of young fans, but it shed the older ones in droves. George, everything you touch will always make squillions, but that's no substitute for a modicum of intellect.

The Last Battle [Le Dernier Combat] (1983, Fr.) ★★★★

Dir/Prod: Luc Besson; *Scr:* Besson, Pierre Jolivet
St: Jolivet, Jean Bouise, Jean Reno, Fritz Wepper

In a blasted post-apocalyptic landscape, people exist in small tribal enclaves and can no longer speak. Jolivet escapes the attentions of a scavenging gang by flying a home-made plane to a ruined town. Ambushed by a lone marauder, he's rescued by a doctor barricaded behind a stockade. The doctor nurses Jolivet back to health, and takes him blindfolded to his other companion: a woman. When the doctor is killed by a freak shower of rocks and the resourceful marauder gets behind the stockade, Jolivet must try to remember the way to get to her first.

This audacious debut from 24-year-old Besson has not received the attention it deserves. The subtle black and white cinematography, jazz rock score by Eric Serra and quirky characters mark it out as the work of a filmmaker with a vision. There is only a single word of dialogue, allowing Besson to concentrate on situations and visuals, creating images that remain with you. A knife thrust into a boot, but no cry of pain issuing forth; a delicate female hand taking a tray of food; instant showers of rocks and fish; and the tension of the marauder waiting, arms folded, as blindfolded Jolivet feels his way towards him. Reno also starred in Besson's *The Big Blue, Nikita* and *Leon* [*The Professional*], none of them sf but all essential viewing.

Koyaanisqatsi (1983, USA) ★★★★★

Dir/Prod: Godfrey Reggio; *Scr:* Reggio, Ron Fricke, Michael Hoenig, Alton Walpole

Francis Coppola championed this virtually uncategorisable film that is not intended as sf, but establishes an almost pure sf-nal sense of wonder through an overload of images and music. There are no actors, no dialogue and no plot, just stunning cinematography as Fricke's camera takes in some of the most incredible natural land formations and geographic wonders of the world before introducing man's influence, building vast cities and transforming the landscape. Philip Glass' ubiquitous score blends orchestral and electronic systems music to create a hypnotic aural backdrop to the image assault. The title is from the Hopi language, meaning 'life out of balance', and the ecological message is an unsubtle criticism of man's destruction of his environment. However, particularly in one mind-blowing hyperdrive segment titled 'The Grid', the cityscapes are presented in such ravishing beauty that it is hard not to see them as examples of human brilliance. The final sequence as an unmanned satellite fragments and spins through the sky (predating similar footage of the doomed shuttles Challenger and Columbia) to a Gregorian-style chorus achieves unbelievable poignancy. The rapid-fire edits, time-lapse photography, slow-motion and speeded-up sequences look overfamiliar today from pop videos and advertising, but this is their point of origin. There is no other cinema experience quite like it, and it is simply required viewing for any sf fan. Reggio made two inferior sequels, *Powaqqatsi* (1988) and *Naqoyqatsi* (2002), but better by far is Fricke's own variant, *Baraka* (1992).

THE TERMINATOR (1984, USA/UK) *****

Dir: James Cameron; *Prod:* Gale Ann Hurd; *Scr:* Cameron, Hurd, loosely based on [originally uncredited] *Outer Limits* screenplays *Soldier* and *Demon With A Glass Hand* by Harlan Ellison
St: Arnold Scwarzenegger, Linda Hamilton, Michael Biehn, Paul Winfield

Sarah Connor's life is boring and uneventful until she sees on

TV that two women with her name have been murdered. Later she is attacked by a huge man wielding an automatic rifle, but a saviour, Reese, helps her to escape. He tells her he's been sent back from the year 2029 to protect her from her attacker, a cybernetic organism called a Terminator, programmed to kill her. Sarah thinks Reese is insane but her disbelief is shattered when the Terminator attacks the police station where she is under protection and blows away most of the force to get at her. Reese rescues her again and they go on the run.

He explains that in 1997 a Satellite AI, Skynet, became (for him)/will become (for her) self-aware, creating a worldwide machine intelligence that launched a nuclear attack on mankind. The Terminators, designed to attack compounds and kill survivors, are virtually indestructible. This one will not stop until she is dead because in 2029 her son John Connor leads the human resistance. Indoctrinated by John's stories of how she taught him survival and leadership skills, Reese hero-worships Sarah, even carrying a battered photograph of her. She asks about John's father, but Reese only knows that he died before the war. She still cannot believe him – she has no lover and little self-confidence – but as they stay ahead of the cyborg she discovers a sense of purpose and determination. She and Reese grow close and make love. In the final show-down the skeletal Terminator, its skin burned away, is blown in half by Reese's home-made explosives but still relentlessly pursues Sarah through an automated factory. With Reese dead, she finally lures it into an industrial press which crushes it.

En route to Mexico, Sarah pulls in for gas. She is pregnant. A young boy takes her photograph – the same one that Reese had – and his father tells her it looks like stormy weather ahead.

The Terminator was a phenomenon, boasting terrific direction, editing, music and action sequences. Former FX man Cameron worked on *Escape From New York* and was art director on *Battle Beyond The Stars* for Roger Corman's legendary New World films (a highly successful exploitation enterprise in the low-budget horror and sf market). He moved into directing with the awful *Piranha II: Flying Killers*. He and partner Hurd developed the story of *The Terminator* and eventually found funding from UK production company Hemdale. The film showed Cameron was clearly an sf fan who knew his stuff. Most of the effects are marvellous, in particular Stan Winston's metal Terminator skeleton. Some are less good, like the kit-on-wires hunter-killer ships, but the whole film cost a paltry $6.5 million, less than most other films' FX alone. Schwarzenegger established his iconic screen persona in a role that suited him like the big leather biker jacket he steals. He was considered for Reese, but the character had too much dialogue. His odd Austrian vowels were perfect for minimal ripostes like 'Fuck you, asshole' and 'I'll be back', his most-quoted movie line, delivered as he leaves the ill-fated police station. Hamilton and Biehn are perfectly cast, striking up fireworks as the cross-time lovers. Cameron's friend from *Piranha II* Lance Henriksen was originally cast as the Terminator, on the basis that it would be designed to look ordinary, and was given a consolation role as a cop. The script deals ingeniously with time paradoxes; the idea that Reese is John Connor's father creates a fascinating loop. Cameron failed to credit Harlan Ellison's *Outer Limits* scripts, although he had mentioned them in interviews as influences; he should have seen the lawsuit coming. Ellison settled for $400,000 damages and a screen credit. With this and its sequel, plus *Aliens* and *The Abyss*, Cameron took over the mantle of king of sf from Ridley Scott.

2010: The Year We Make Contact (1984, USA) ★★★

Dir/Prod/Scr: Peter Hyams
St: Roy Scheider, John Lithgow, Helen Mirren, Bob Balaban

The sequel to *2001: A Space Odyssey* tries hard to recapture the sprawling scope and thematic range of the original, but while it's by no means bad, it was always going to fall short. *Auteur* Kubrick set the bar impossibly high for a *metteur en scene* like Hyams to reach, and despite the day-to-day involvement of Arthur C. Clarke (who appears in a cameo, on a bench outside the White House), *2010* cannot escape the giant shadow cast by its monolithic predecessor. The cast and FX are especially good, but by forcing *2001*'s enigmatic odyssey into a literal continuation, it became just another space movie. Still, Hyams certainly did a far better job than his previous sf dumbbells *Capricorn One* and *Outland* would have suggested.

Dune (1984, USA) ★★

Dir: David Lynch; *Prod:* Raffaella De Laurentiis; *Scr:* Lynch, from the novel by Frank Herbert
St: Kyle MacLachlan, Jürgen Prochnow, Kenneth McMillan, Francesca Annis

In the year 10,191, the spice Melange is the most valuable commodity in the Universe, found only on the planet Arrakis. Duke Leto Atreides controls spice mines for Emperor Shaddam IV, but gigantic sandworms on Arrakis make mining dangerous. Arrakis' desert tribe, the Fremen, hold a prophecy that a messiah will come and merge with the universal consciousness. Leto's son Paul is being tested by his mother Jessica's shadowy galactic sisterhood, the Bene Gesserit. Emperor Shaddam helps evil House Harkonnen to defeat House Atreides. Using a traitor, the Harkonnens disable their defence shields and attack. Leto is killed and Paul and Jessica face death in the desert, but his powers enable them to escape. They live among the Fremen, who make Jessica their leader. Her daughter Alia is also born with special powers. Paul leads the Fremen against the Harkonnens, harnessing the power of the sandworms to defeat them. Paul proves he is the Kwizatz Haderach, the messiah who can finally cause rain to fall on barren Arrakis.

The weight of expectation on Lynch's shoulders from De Laurentiis' colossal $50 million budget resulted in a hellish year-long shoot in desert heat and poor Mexican air. The surreal, experimental Lynch (*Eraserhead*, *Blue Velvet*) was sunk having to adapt an epic, linear novel. Dino's daughter Raffaella and Lynch were too inexperienced to cope with the complex effects, huge sets and over a thousand-strong crew, and the production nearly fell apart. *Star Wars* FX genius John Dykstra walked off the film, and cinematographer Freddie Francis finished early.

Lynch's first cut ran for four hours. He had to trim it to 137 minutes, thereby losing the thread of the complex novel. *Dune* was very poorly received. The consensus was that it was confused, camp and far less than the sum of its parts. Some good touches including Victorian steam-iron chic production design by Tony Masters (*2001*) and McMillan's turn as the disgusting, Lynchian Baron Harkonnen could not overcome incoherence and some ropey mechanical and optical effects. Fans of the novel were incensed, particularly with the tacked-on Hollywood ending of rain on Arrakis. The music score by MOR rock band Toto didn't help either. It was a critical and financial disaster, and nearly took De Laurentiis' DEG Films under. Lynch never revisited sf. He said, 'I really went pretty insane on that picture … *Dune* took me off at the knees.'

Starman (1984, USA) ★★★

Dir: John Carpenter; *Prod:* Larry J. Franco, Barry Bernardi; *Scr:* Bruce A. Evans and Raynold Gideon
St: Karen Allen, Jeff Bridges, Charles Martin Smith, Richard Jaeckel

An alien ship intercepts the Voyager probe and accepts its invitation to Earth, but is shot down. At the home of recently widowed Jenny Hayden the non-corporeal alien uses DNA from a lock of her husband's hair to reconstruct him. Understandably, this freaks Jenny out, especially as it doesn't have the hang of using a human body. The two embark on an alien/human bonding trip across America, but the military are on their trail, as is nice-guy SETI (Search for Extra-Terrestrial Intelligence) scientist Mark Shermin. The Starman must reach

Arizona in three days to be picked up by his people at the site of an old meteor crater, or he'll die.

Sugary but enjoyable *CE3K* meets *E.T.* chick-flick, as far from *The Thing* as you can get. As ever with Spielbergian scifantastifiction there are gaping holes: Why does the Starman not just get his buddies to pick him up somewhere nearer? Why did he only bring a few glowing balls? The film veers into Lucas' no-go area of power over life and death, as the Star Christ resurrects a deer on a hunter's car, and then Jenny herself (so why is *he* dying?). He also makes her pregnant, setting up a sequel that never came. Bridges' performance was Oscar-nominated, which is odd as he mainly does Jeffrey's chicken-walk from *Blue Velvet*. Allen is good as usual. The opening where Jenny gets drunk and weeps while watching a home movie of her and hubby singing 'Dreams' gets us on her side straightaway. Jack Nitzsche's lush Synclavier score is simple but beautiful. The reflective alien sphere is almost identical to one in Mike Gray's *Wavelength*, released the same year. Again, Hollywood acknowledges that aliens will not be welcome, despite the invitation. Shermin asks 'Who is the missionary and who are the savages?' but we've known the answer since the 50s.

Back To The Future (1985, USA) ★★★★

Dir: Robert Zemeckis; *Prod:* Bob Gale, Neil Canton; *Scr:* Zemeckis, Gale
St: Michael J. Fox, Christopher Lloyd, Lea Thompson, Crispin Glover

The best mainstream time-travel movie, and it'll probably remain so until someone films Robert Silverberg's classic novel *Up The Line*. It doesn't strictly belong here, but just in case you've never seen it, see it. Also see the second (lemme guess, *BTTF II*? You got it …), which is darker and almost as good. Frankly, I wouldn't bother with the third for-cash-only outing. And while I'm in the mood, check out *Bill And Ted's Excellent Adventure* and *Bill And Ted's Bogus Journey*. Both fun, clever time-travel scenarios that found a pre-*Matrix* use for Keanu Reeves. The second is better, and has a great *Star Trek* in-gag.

Brazil (1985, UK) *****

Dir: Terry Gilliam; *Prod:* Arnon Milchan; *Scr:* Gilliam, Tom Stoppard, Charles McKeown
St: Jonathan Pryce, Robert De Niro, Kim Greist, Michael Palin

In The Ministry, Sam Lowry goes about his menial office job. He fantasises about flying through the sky, battling an emor-mous Samurai-demon and baby-faced minions of darkness, and finding the girl of his dreams. When he sees the same girl in The Ministry he burrows his way into the bureaucratic machinery to access her file. This leads to complications, exac-erbated by a case of mistaken identity between terrorist plumber Harry Tuttle and dream girl Jill's neighbour Harry Buttle, arrested because of a clerical glitch. As Lowry crashes into Jill's life and becomes more daring in his pursuit, he comes to the attention of Ministry minions who'll stop at nothing to curb his individual display of non-conformity.

A kind of sf *Citizen Kane, Brazil* became a *cause célèbre* when Gilliam and Universal head Sid Sheinberg fought a bitter battle over its release. Former sixth Monty Python member Gilliam rejected studio changes to his vision, regarding them as mindless butchery. They hated the downbeat ending and recut the film to make it less enigmatic and more marketable. Gilliam's tireless efforts to publicise the conflict, including a full-page advert in *Variety*, gave Hollywood's own David vs Goliath story a huge profile. In desperation, he sneaked out his print and screened it for the LA Film Critics circle. They gave it several awards at their influential pre-Oscars ceremony, including Best Film, Best Director and Best Script. This in effect forced Universal to release Gilliam's cut … which took less than $10 million at the box office.

Yet again, the dilemma of intelligent, left-field sf reared its ugly head. Why gamble on it if it's destined not to find an audience? But if you do gamble, the creative vision should be upheld and not diluted. *Brazil* is a true one-off, a variant of *1984*, but more ironic and deliriously inventive. Sam is Winston Smith reborn with an oedipus complex, projecting his embarrassing desires for his mother onto the feisty Jill, who rejects his advances until she gives herself to him in his mother's home, wearing her clothes. Indeed, she may well be a figment of his tortured imagination, or an escape from real torture at the hands of the men from the Ministry. Gilliam's vision is like Philip K. Dick directed by Kubrick as a Python sketch. At the end, Sam has retreated so far into his mind that his torturer is told 'He's got away from us, Jack.' Gilliam's all-or-nothing war of the individual against The System is mirrored in his efforts to save his creation, chronicled in Jack Mathews' book *The Battle Of Brazil*.

Lifeforce (1985, UK) ★★

Dir: Tobe Hooper; *Prod:* Menahem Golan, Yoram Globus; *Scr:* Dan O'Bannon, Don Jakoby
St: Steve Railsback, Peter Firth, Frank Finlay, Mathilda May

An insane oddball that probably should be clucking among the turkeys, but for some crazy reason I have time for it. Loosely based on Colin Wilson's novel *The Space Vampires* and directed by the variable Hooper (*Texas Chainsaw Massacre, Poltergeist*), it concerns the discovery, by European Space Agency probe ship *Churchill*, of an alien craft and its deadly occupants in the wake of Halley's Comet. There is much eyeful of naked astro vampyrette May as she literally sucks the life out of poor saps who can't resist her charms (well, could you?). London descends into chaos as its citizens are reborn as lifesucking hordes and Firth's SAS Colonel (yeah, right) tries wimpfully to deal with the situation. But, but, but … some nice effects (exploring the immense alien ship); interesting, if variable prosthetic work (bodies sucked into dry husks) and great performances (just kidding) make *Lifeforce* required viewing, if only to wonder at the gobsmacking *chutzpah* of it all.

The Fly (1986, USA) ★★★★

Dir: David Cronenberg; *Prod:* Stuart Cornfeld; *Scr:* Cronenberg, Charles Edward Pogue, from a story by George Langelaan
St: Jeff Goldblum, Geena Davis, John Getz

Gawky scientist Seth Brundle invents a matter transmitter, which he reveals to cute journalist Veronica. She begins work on an exclusive and they become lovers. He tests the process by putting himself through the telepod, but unknown to him a fly shares the experience, and he fuses with it at the molecular level. He disintegrates into the hybrid 'Brundlefly', shedding body parts, walking on ceilings and vomiting bile over food before ingesting it. This is too much for Veronica, who is pregnant with his child. When she tries to terminate it he kidnaps her. Her boss and ex-lover Stathis Borans tries to rescue her from his lab, but Brundlefly douses him with corrosive vomit before placing Veronica in the pod in order to fuse with her and the unborn child. Borans shoots the cables and instead the creature fuses with the metal pod. It drags itself to Veronica and places the shotgun to its head. She puts it out of its misery.

Cronenberg's cerebral, creepy remake of Kurt Neumann's 1958 original added a welcome scientific rationale and a touch of class. Easily his most profitable movie, it confirmed his status as a leading sf writer/director. He wrings every last drop of pathos out of the doomed creature, while maintaining his usual gloopy excess. Chris Walas' make-up and mechanical effects deserve a mention, unlike his uninspired sequel, *The Fly II* (1988).

Aliens (1986, USA) ★★★★

Dir: James Cameron; *Prod:* Gale Ann Hurd; *Scr:* Cameron, from a story by David Giler and Walter Hill
St: Sigourney Weaver, Michael Biehn, Paul Reiser, Lance Henriksen

After drifting in space for 57 years, Ripley's shuttle is picked up. She is brought to Earth, where because of Einsteinian relativity, her daughter has grown old and died. Her story is not immediately believed, because the planet the Nostromo landed on is now a thriving terraformed colony, Acheron. Sure enough, contact is lost and Ripley is pressured into going back with a team of swaggering marines to investigate. They find the colonists have been massacred, they're surrounded by hundreds of aliens and have to fight their way out. They rescue a little girl, Newt, whom Ripley takes personal responsibility for getting out alive.

'This Time It's War!' *Aliens* is half Vietnam movie, half *Starship Troopers*. After a slow start mimicking the pace of the first film, it becomes a flat-out actionfest as typified by Heinlein's novel. The production design fetishises space hardware: there are drop ships, battletanks and very large pulse rifles everywhere. There is also the Powerloader Waldo that Ripley wears for her climactic encounter with the alien Queen. Her line 'Get away from her you BITCH!' is another Cameron tough-guy catchphrase. His personality is in every frame, which is both good and bad.

My problem with *Aliens* is that it's a very good movie, but it's not a good sequel. I really wanted the second film to take place on Earth, and Jones to be the carrier. *Starship Troopers* was just the wrong direction for me. I never bought the idea that Ripley would go back to the planet. Also, the company knew about the alien(s) as they programmed Ash to protect it/them, so they knew the dangers of colonisation. Another problem is that on paper the odds are so great that there is simply no way the humans can win without the need first to diminish the potency of the alien threat. Cameron, Stan Winston's effects team plus the cinematographer and editor may have worked miracles making only six alien suits look like hundreds, but the all-powerful killing machine from the first film is diluted into slower, smaller, less effective *mortal* creatures. Cameron reprises many elements from *Alien*, such as the final countdown to self-destruct and the company android (this time benevolent), but never approaches Scott's sf sense of wonder.

Weaver got $1 million (after $35,000 for *Alien*) and was the key to the film being made. Cameron intertwines all manner of motherhood symbolism for Ripley, with she and the alien Queen two sides of the same coin, each trying to protect their young. The alien lifecycle was amended to show the Queen as the source of the egg sacs.

Two further sequels were little more than breakthrough projects for directors and vanity projects for the star. Weaver's influence grew, and the films experimented with alien physiology and mentality to a detrimental level. The third, *Alien*[3] (1992) was directed by pop video whizzkid David Fincher, later to make the magnificent *The Game* (1997) and *Fight Club* (1999). Set on a prison planet, it was a grimy, downbeat film populated by grotesques that offered little to fans of the first two. The fourth, *Alien: Resurrection* (1997), was handed to French visual stylist Jean-Pierre Jeunet, who with Marc Caro directed cult hits *Delicatessen* (1991) and *City Of Lost Children* (1997). This production mixed alien and human physiology in a manner at once repulsive, idiotic and schmaltzy. The human/alien 'baby' has to be seen to be disbelieved.

Robocop (1987, USA) ★★★★

Dir: Paul Verhoeven; *Prod:* Arne Schmidt; *Scr:* Ed Neumeier, Michael Miner
St: Peter Weller, Nancy Allen, Miguel Ferrer, Kurtwood Smith

In near-future Detroit, the streets are a deadly battleground and the police, run by OmniConsumer Products, are losing. Patrol cop Murphy is shot to pieces by vicious racketeer Clarence Boddicker's gang, and what's left of him is salvaged by ambitious Bob Morton for an experimental project to build an android supercop. Corporate exec Dick Jones is furious with Morton because his own robot cop project, ED-209, has gone disastrously wrong. Murphy is reborn as a super-human, incorruptible law-enforcing cyborg, and Jones wants rid of him. Robocop goes after Boddicker, but, unknown to

Morton, Jones has had a hand in his programming and is in league with the enemy ...

Verhoeven came to international notice with a series of films made in his native Holland including *Soldier Of Orange*, *Spetters* and the exceptional *The Fourth Man*. Frank and explicit, they established Verhoeven's reputation as a director without a restraining bolt. For his first American film he found the perfect script to suit his cavalier style, a razor-sharp sf satire with lashings of ultraviolence and cutting black humour. He gleefully puts the boot into everything from corporate capitalism to the superficial pomposity of TV news ('You give us three minutes, we'll give you the world.') Weller and Allen make a great leading couple and Smith steals the movie as the deliriously evil Boddicker. An adult sf film in every sense, *Robocop* is a landmark that represents a kind of bookend for the most brightly burning ten-year period in sf movie history.

Predator (1987, USA) ★★★½

Dir: John McTiernan; *Prod:* John Davis, Lawrence Gordon, Joel Silver; *Scr:* Jim Thomas and John Thomas
St: Arnold Schwarzenegger, Carl Weathers, Elpidia Carillo

McTiernan (*Die Hard*) turned an old pulp magazine scenario into an exciting sf action thriller. Major 'Dutch' Schaefer's elite commando company runs into big trouble on a stealth mission in the Amazon jungle when they find themselves the prey of an alien big-game hunter. His men are picked off one by one, ratcheting up the tension until finally it's down (of course) to alien vs Arnie. The creature design by Stan Winston is impressive, with dreadlocks and a visage like a crab's innards. Its near-invisible camouflage and thermal-vision POV are striking effects (the latter similar to *Wolfen*). Add to that an awesome display of hardware firepower that decimates half the jungle, plus Arnie on best monosyllabic macho form, and you have an sf thriller that delivers. A 1990 sequel, directed by Stephen Hopkins (*Lost in Space*, *24*) isn't quite in the same league but does feature a nice visual gag of an Alien skull in the Predator's Trophy room.

The Hidden (1988, USA) ★★★★

Dir: Jack Sholder; *Prod:* Robert Shaye, Gerald T. Olson, Michael Meltzer; *Scr:* Bob Hunt
St: Kyle MacLachlan, Michael Nouri, Claudia Christian, William Boyett

A bodysnatching alien with punk attitude and a penchant for sex, fast cars and rock 'n' roll switches hosts whenever the old one is used up. On its trail is bemused policeman Tom Beck, who knows only that seemingly ordinary, unconnected people are exhibiting similar extreme criminal traits, and FBI agent Lloyd Gallagher, who knows more than he's letting on. When Beck runs a check on Gallagher and finds he was killed on duty, he isn't prepared for what he's about to discover.

Great fun, low-budget cracker from Sholder, who also directed the superior TV movie *12:01* (1993), which shares many similarities with *Groundhog Day*. Fresh-faced MacLachlan (*Dune*) has a ball playing the eccentric Lloyd, a virtual template for Agent Dale Cooper in *Twin Peaks*. Christian appears as a stripper, a must-see for *Babylon 5* fans. Boyett is terrific as a middle-aged heart patient taken over by the alien. Whether shooting up a music store, playing his music LOUD in a diner, or rushing off after a Ferrari ('I *want* that car!'), he's hypnotically watchable. If you like fast-paced sf with humour, a clever plot and plenty of action, this is a treat.

They Live (1988, USA) ★★★½

Dir: John Carpenter; *Prod:* Larry J. Franco; *Scr:* Frank Armitage (Carpenter), from the story *Eight O'Clock In The Morning* by Ray Nelson
St: Roddy Piper, Keith David, Meg Foster

Drifter John Nada gets a construction job in LA and witnesses a heavy-handed police raid on a local church mission. Nosing around, he finds a hidden box containing sunglasses. These extraordinary lenses reveal the truth – society has been infiltrated by ugly aliens, with TV and print media carrying a series of subliminal instructions: 'CONSUME', 'OBEY', 'MARRY AND REPRODUCE', 'DO NOT QUESTION AUTHORITY', and my favourite, 'REWARD INDIFFER- ENCE'. Nada enlists the help of co-worker Frank to join the underground resistance attempting to jam the alien signal and alert society to the danger in its midst. But the underground has in turn been infiltrated by human traitors ...

They Live satirises 80s 'Greed is good' Reaganomics and Thatcherism, substituting aliens for the parasitic business/ political elite growing richer and more powerful on the backs of the working classes. It also has a go at the complicity of the mass media, as the alien/government partnership uses TV to keep people compliant and docile. The message may be heavy, but the tone is pop-culture light, from the casting of wrestler 'Rowdy' Roddy Piper as Nada – literally, 'nothing' – to the dialogue ('I'm here to chew bubblegum and kick ass, and I'm all out of bubblegum.'), to the aliens' grinning grey skulls. There's a memorable slapstick fight when Frank won't try on the glasses and he and Nada hammer each other for five minutes, in a homage to the punch up in John Ford's *The Quiet Man*. The distrust of political systems seen in *Dark Star* and *Escape From New York* is again evident, and *TL* fits into a rich vein of paranoid texts including *The X-Files* and *The Matrix*. A subversive, slightly demented B-movie, it's Carpenter's last film worthy of his name.

Miracle Mile (1988, USA) ★★★

Dir/Scr: Steve De Jarnatt; *Prod:* John Daly, Derek Gibson, Graham Cottle
St: Anthony Edwards, Mare Winningham, John Agar

Having overslept and missed his date, Edwards goes in the early hours to the diner on LA's Miracle Mile where she works, but she's gone. Outside he answers a nagging public phone. A desperate, sobbing voice tells him the bombs are in the air and he must prepare for the end. When he protests, the caller realises he has a wrong number. There is a commotion, followed by shots. Another voice comes on the line, tells him to forget what he's heard and hangs up. He believes he's been given advance warning of a nuclear strike, and he has 50 minutes to find his girl and get out of LA. Soon panic spreads and the city becomes a free-for-all as the veneer of civilisation is torn apart in the desperate stampede to leave.

MM begins as romantic drama, then segues into sf/horror via one of the best screen telephone calls. A couple of inexplicable plot developments and some uneven acting don't spoil a fascinating premise, and the ending thankfully avoids Hollywood cop-out. De Jarnatt also directed the $10 million flop *Cherry 2000* (1985), starring Melanie Griffith as a futuristic female scavenger.

The Abyss (1989, USA) ***

Dir/Scr: James Cameron; *Prod:* Gale Ann Hurd
St: Ed Harris, Mary Elizabeth Mastrantonio, Michael Biehn

In an uneasy alliance, a Navy SEAL unit and the crew of underwater oil workers attempt to rescue a US nuclear submarine. When they discover an alien lifeform in the ocean depths, the SEAL commander flips and tries to nuke it. It's down to chief oilman Bud Brigman to dive to insane depths and disarm the warhead.

Cameron's technology fetish reached its zenith as he piled the hardware in front of the human characters. An incredibly hazardous underwater shoot left many trailing in its wake, with furious actors and crew blasting the director's megalomania. Harris refused to speak about his experience or to work with Cameron again. The Brigmans' troubled marriage was informed by Cameron and Hurd's own divorce. The obligatory special edition of Cameron's cut is a longer and better film than the theatrical release, with a *Day The Earth Stood Still*-type warning as the aliens hold huge tidal waves suspended to threaten against nuclear force.

3: Fin De Siècle (1990–1999)

'In the modern era ... you can put virtually any image convincingly on the screen, and of course the immediate casualty (is) any other aspect of the film.'

Dan O'Bannon (Screenwriter/Director)

In the 90s, developments in computer technology gave an unprecedented level of sophistication and realism to sf movie effects, but, as O'Bannon points out, they had a tendency to be overused with the result that the spectacle swamped the stories. Whether it was lightning-fast or lumbering dinosaurs, city-sized alien ships going down in flames, giant insect bugs sucking out brains, little green Martians filleting the President, skyscraper-level traffic jams or the path of bullets dodged by computer-game heroes, CGI offered sf movies an incredible spectacle that would have given Wells and Verne heart attacks. The spirit of the age in the countdown to the new millennium was that there was no spirit of the age. Everything was much as it had been, with flawed, unheroic heroes and resigned, gallows-style humour. It wasn't until the end of the decade that a new mythical Hero arose; the sleeper who awakes, the farmboy who defeats the Empire, the computer nerd who gets to see, as Burroughs said, what's really on the end of every fork.

Total Recall (1990, USA) ★★

Dir: Paul Verhoeven; *Prod:* Buzz Feitshans, Ronald Shusett; *Scr:* Shusett, Dan O'Bannon, Gary Goldman
St: Arnold Schwarzenegger, Rachel Ticotin, Sharon Stone, Ronny Cox

Verhoeven had just made a great movie (*Robocop*), Schwarzenegger was on a roll with the *Terminator* franchise, Shusett and O'Bannon had collaborated on *Alien* and their script was taken from the short story *We Can Remember It For You Wholesale*, by Philip K. Dick. Several big-name directors including David Cronenberg had been attached to the project. But somehow, it all went so wrong. Verhoeven overindulged his puerility; the tone careers wildly between slapstick, camp and macho thriller; the screenwriters regurgitated Dick's story as spam, and Arnie mangled even the most basic dialogue. *TR* is a crude cartoon featuring cardboard characters, laughable 'science', and some amazingly ropey effects. There are a few nice Dickian touches (Arnie's fat female tourist disguise, the cheeky automated Johnnycab taxi, the attempts to penetrate Quaid's illusion), but the rest is like watching an out-of-control bus bearing down on a group of pensioners. The film's tag line was: 'Someone stole his brain. Now he wants it back.' T-shirts appeared with it changed to: 'Someone stole his brain. And he didn't notice.'

Terminator 2: Judgment Day (1991, USA) *****

Dir/Prod: James Cameron; *Scr:* Cameron, William Wisher
St: Arnold Schwarzenegger, Linda Hamilton, Edward Furlong, Robert Patrick

In 1997 the machines send back an ultra-sophisticated T1000 Terminator, which can assume any form it touches, to kill John Connor. In response, the humans send an altered T800; the same model that tried to kill Sarah in 1984. John is a 13-year-old delinquent and Sarah is in a secure mental institution after trying to sabotage Skynet. The T800 saves John from the T1000, and together they break Sarah out of the asylum. They have to stay ahead of the T1000, get armed and stop Miles Dyson, the mastermind behind Skynet, before the events triggering the apocalypse are irrevocably in place.

That true rarity, a *great* sequel; the best since *Mad Max 2*. SuperstArnie was too big to play the bad guy, so he returned as the *good* Terminator, reprogrammed to obey John Connor. Weasel-faced Patrick is eerily menacing as the 'liquid metal' T1000, aided by new digital CG 'morphing' techniques, allowing an object or person to blend seamlessly into another form. Shots of the T1000 taking great shotgun blasts and the holes simply closing up, or being blown in half and reintegrating, were truly amazing. Like many sequels, it recycles the original plot, but it also cleverly expands the original's themes. Sarah is insanely driven; with her hard body and rigorous discipline she's more machine-like than the T800, which assumes a fatherly role in John's life. John also gets the best toy a kid could want. Although John's wild he is also principled, and won't allow the T800 to kill humans. The T800 learns to empathise with human emotions (the only grinding false note), and sacrifices itself in a molten furnace so that its technology can't be found and abused. Arnie gets another memorable catchphrase ('Hasta la vista, baby') and another Lear jet for his trouble.

One of the best scenes only surfaced in Cameron's now-obligatory Director's Cut: after being beaten in her cell, Sarah wakes to find Reese, warning her to keep it together. She follows him out of the cell, down a long corridor and opens a door onto a bright LA day. She watches her other, 'normal' self with a group of children in a playground. She shakes the fence and shouts, but a blinding light engulfs downtown LA and the blast wave spreads to vapourise the playground and herself. I'm normally wary of dream/hallucination scenes, but this knocked me out.

Until The End Of The World [Bis Ans Ende Der Welt] (1991, Ger./Fr./Aust.) *½

Dir: Wim Wenders; *Prod:* Jonathan T. Taplin, Ulrich Felsberg; *Scr:* Michael Almereyda, Peter Carey, Wenders, from an idea by Solveig Dommartin and Wenders
St: Dommartin, William Hurt, Sam Neill, Max Von Sydow

Smitten Claire travels the world pursuing slippery con man

Sam. Along for the ride at various points are her estranged partner Gene, an inept German private eye and a French bank robber who inexplicably gives her his loot. In remote Coober Pedy, Australia, she helps Sam and his father process images from a special camera that allow his blind mother (Jeanne Moreau) to see. After her death, Claire and Sam become obsessed with the camera's ability to record dreams. They descend into an existential funk until he goes on walkabout and she is put in cold turkey by Gene. She becomes an astronaut on board an eco-satellite. And, er, that's it. Wenders is known for his ponderous, lyrical narratives (*Paris, Texas*; *Wings Of Desire*), but if his intention was to create a mindbending Lynchian dreamstate, he failed miserably. Characters' actions are often incomprehensible, especially why so many guys run around after pain-in-the-ass Claire. This incoherent farrago is doubly infuriating because certain scenes suggest the possibility of something much better. Subplots simply vanish; for example, the shooting down of an Indian nuclear satellite that may cause the end of the world, and the reason Sam steals opals. This may be because the version I saw runs 158 minutes, whereas Wenders' original 'vision' ran 280 – four hours and 40 minutes! I'll give the European DVD of the Director's Cut a miss, as it's already taken up 2½ hours of my life that I want back.

Jurassic Park (1993, USA) ★★½

Dir: Steven Spielberg; *Prod:* Kathleen Kennedy, Gerald R. Molen; *Scr:* Michael Crichton, David Koepp, from Crichton's novel
St: Sam Neill, Laura Dern, Jeff Goldblum, Richard Attenborough

Imagine if dinosaurs could be recreated using fossil DNA. John Hammond has done so, and he's about to open up his Costa Rican island as a spectacular living history museum. But wait! There's a problem. The dinos are revolting and the security isn't up to scratch. Paleontologists Neill and Dern and a couple of obligatory brats must stay ahead of the deadly Velociraptors if they want to avoid being lunch …

More popcorn from sf's biggest kids Spielberg and Crichton, whose novel extracted DNA from *Westworld* (robot theme park to dino Disneyland). One character says 'How can we possibly have the slightest idea what to expect?' We know *exactly* what to expect: formulaic narrative, irritating characters (Goldblum's on another mission to deliver dumb wisecracks) and annoying inconsistencies. The scientists are dealing with the most fearsome beasts ever to stride the Earth, but with inadequate weapons and no fail-safe measures; the technicians vanish (where'd they go?) at the first sign of danger, etc. It's undeniably well made, but with a vacuum at its centre. If that doesn't bother you, there's much to enjoy. Chiefly the effects, which are much better than the wring-out-the-cash sequels, using groundbreaking CGI to convey the full amazement of prehistoric creatures in our midst.

Johnny Mnemonic (1995, USA) ★★

Dir: Robert Longo; *Prod:* Don Carmody; *Scr:* William Gibson
St: Keanu Reeves, Dina Meyer, Ice T, Takeshi Kitano

A movie from the sf literature 'cyberpunk' wave, scripted disappointingly by Gibson, whose 1984 novel *Neuromancer* began it all. Canadian artist Longo proves it takes a bit more than a fine-art sensibility to direct a movie, and Reeves rehearses his career-making *Matrix* role with a fraction of the impact. Not a total dingo, but too superficial to stay longer in the mind than last week's shopping list.

Strange Days (1995, USA) ★★★★

Dir: Kathryn Bigelow; *Prod:* James Cameron, Steven-Charles Jaffe; *Scr:* Cameron, Jay Cocks, from a story by Cameron
St: Ralph Fiennes, Angela Bassett, Juliette Lewis, Tom Sizemore

This semi-cyberpunk gem from Cameron and another of his many wives is altogether more successful than the aforementioned *Johnny Mnemonic*. Bigelow has forged an unusual career in the male domains of horror and action thrillers (*Near Dark*, *Point Break*, *Blue Steel*), and here she does a great job of delivering a visually rich and complex narrative with a punch. Sleazy ex-cop Lenny Nero comes into possession of a memory tape made by a murdered friend. Her tape shows the assassination of black political rapper Jeriko-One by renegade LAPD patrolmen. Nero is now their number one target as he tries to bring the tape to senior police attention, all set against the half-party, half-riot of the Year 2000 celebrations. Cameron's scenario expands to include one of the most unrequited romances ever (Nero virtually lives for and in tapes of old girlfriend Faith), and much debate about the ethics of recording super-realistic experiences. *Strange Days* arrived with synchronicity at the time of the notorious O.J. Simpson case, but died nonetheless. That's a real shame as it offers classy high-octane sf thrills and some amazing POV camerawork. The opening sequence, a subjective tape made by an armed robber on a botched heist, is worth the price alone.

12 Monkeys (1995, USA) ****

Dir: Terry Gilliam; *Prod:* Charles (Chuck) Roven; *Scr:* David Webb Peoples, Janet Peoples, inspired by the film *La Jetée*, by Chris Marker
St: Bruce Willis, Madeleine Stowe, Brad Pitt, Christopher Plummer

In the bleak post-apocalyptic world of 2035, James Cole is a prisoner sent back to 1996 to discover the origin of the virus that wiped out most of humanity, and the role of an obscure organisation, The Army Of The 12 Monkeys. However, faulty equipment sends him to 1990, and he is incarcerated in an asylum. Case psychiatrist Kathryn Railly feels that she has seen him somewhere. He is befriended by paranoid idealist Jeffrey Goines, who helps him to escape but he is too drugged to get far. Cole mysteriously disappears from his secure cell. In 2035, under interrogation, he wonders if he really *is* insane. Redeployed to the past, he is pitched into a WWI trench battle, and is shot in the leg before jumping forward again.

In 1996, he abducts Railly and forces her to help him track down The Army Of The 12 Monkeys, a motley bunch led by the crazy Goines. Cole suspects that he triggered a self-fulfilling prophecy six years earlier by giving Goines the idea of the virus, the source of which must be Goines' father, a leading virologist. When the Army carries out its mission though, it is to protest Goines senior's vivisection work by liberating the animals from Philadelphia zoo. Cole realises that the future information about the virus is false, generated by his own erroneous data. He wants to remain in the present and take his chances with Kathryn, but is plagued by doubts: could he be insane and imagining all this? If so, how could Kathryn have removed an antique bullet from his leg? How can she have a WWI photograph of a man who looks just like him? And why does he keep dreaming of a boyhood trauma, witnessing a man being gunned down at an airport, with a woman who looks like a blonde version of Kathryn?

Based on *La Jetée*'s central conceit of a man witnessing his own death, *TM*'s blackly comic sf love story is a complex labyrinth of switchbacks, paradoxes and time-shifts. Cole meets Kathryn in 1990, but for him 1996 is the past and his present is 40 years later. The dark dystopia of 2035 is that of *Brazil* after 50 years of decline. Lions and bears roam snowy Philadelphia, humans live in bleak dungeons and individual freedoms are non-existent. The look is also pure Gilliam: a weird blend of modern and Victorian retro-machinery, like the floating ball of TV screens and cameras. Cole is a typical Gilliam/Dick ordinary Joe; like Sam Lowry, he is forced to keep trying to make sense of his life and his world, uncertain of his status and his sanity. Action man Willis excels in an unac-customed role and gives the film a solid centre. Gilliam emphasises his dislocation with the usual extreme distorted close-ups, odd angles, manic camera tilts and swoops.

Co-screenwriter David Webb Peoples also co-wrote *Blade*

Runner. Early test screenings were disastrous, but Gilliam ruled out wholesale changes and was proven right. The lure of Willis and Pitt, plus an effective marketing campaign, helped *12 Monkeys* to take $160 million worldwide.

Mars Attacks! (1996, USA) ★★★½

Dir: Tim Burton; *Prod:* Burton, Larry Franco; *Scr:* Jonathan Gems
St: Jack Nicholson, Pierce Brosnan, Lukas Haas, Glenn Close

Hilarious combination of *Earth Vs. The Flying Saucers* and the Topps bubblegum cards. Burton's acid-tinged spoof comes with some priceless moments. The opening with a farmer saying to another that his burgers smell good before a herd of blazing cattle comes over the hill is topped only by the massacre of the welcoming party. This is a gut-bustingly funny inversion of *The Day The Earth Stood Still*, and one which is repeated when the Martians gleefully go along with the bizarre pacifist theory that they perceived the release of a dove as a threat. The Martians are pure cartoon grinning skulls with bulbous brains and a Nazi sense of humour. They play skittles with the Easter Island heads, etch their own faces on Mount Rushmore, transplant Sarah Jessica Parker's dog's head onto hers and vice-versa, and gleefully atomise Michael J. Fox. I mean, what more could you possibly want?

Space Truckers (1996, USA/Ire.) ★★½

Dir: Stuart Gordon; *Prod:* Peter Newman, Greg Johnson, Ted Mann, Gordon, Mary Breen-Farrelly; *Scr:* Mann
St: Dennis Hopper, Stephen Dorff, Debi Mazar, Charles Dance

Interstellar trucker John Canyon is fired for late delivery of genetically altered square pigs. He sets out for Earth with a consignment of plastic sex dolls, plus passengers Mike and Nicki. His ship is hijacked by space pirate Macanudo, desperate to extract revenge on his old boss E.J. Saggs, ruler of Earth. The cargo he's after is not sex dolls, but a lethal army of biomechanoid robots that he created for Saggs. He's also desperate for female contact, but as he's had to rebuild himself and his, er, equipment is faulty (for him, a screw is literally that), Nicki doesn't see the attraction.

Engaging cornball spoof boasting some quality effects, particularly the design of the pirate ship USS *Regalia* and the biomechanoids, by Hajime Soroyama. Hopper and Dorff look uneasy throughout, but Vernon Wells, Mohawk biker Wez in *Mad Max 2*, makes a welcome appearance as a pirate. Gordon, who made his name with exploitation horrors like *Re-animator* and his money from the original story for *Honey, I Shrunk The Kids*, directs in journeyman style. The opening sequence, as the robots wipe out a heavily armed lunar fortress, suggests a far better movie.

Contact (1997, USA) ★★★★

Dir: Robert Zemeckis, *Prod:* Zemeckis, Steve Starkey, *Scr:* James V. Hart, Michael Goldenberg, based on the novel by Carl Sagan
St: Jodie Foster, Matthew McConaughey, Tom Skerritt, Angela Bassett

Evangelistic astronomer Ellie Arroway intercepts signals indicating alien intelligence. Once they are deciphered there's no doubt. She eventually gets to visit them, using a machine built to their schematics. Or does she …?

At last, a film that proves it's possible for me to love an sf movie with an exaggerated religious sensibility and a pompously inflated sense of itself, and proves that Hollywood can deliver mainstream science fiction. Unlike *CE3K*, I can forgive *Contact*'s preachiness because at its core is a solid sf movie with ideas and ideals, instead of an escapist Disney fantasy. And, like *Solaris*, it dares to suggest that human subjectivity may transcend scientific objectivity, asking questions without need of answers. It feels realistic in the reactions of scientific, political, military and religious organisations to the prospect of first contact, and posits our subjectivity by offering differing possibilities: the signals could be a hoax by a multi-billionaire and Ellie may not have contacted anything except her own emptiness, need and longing. She is the adult version of *CE3K*'s Roy Neary – he gets to go with the alien kiddiewinks, she gets to doubt her senses. The opening CG pull-out from a point on Earth right out into the cosmos is a great way to establish the sheer awestruck wonder that Ellie feels, that we all may feel when faced with the prospect of not being alone in the Universe. See it.

Cube (1997, Can.) ★★★½

Dir: Vincenzo Natali; *Prod:* Mehra Meh, Betty Orr; *Scr:* André Bijelic, Natali, Graeme Manson
St: Nicole deBoer, Nicky Guadagni, David Hewlett

Six strangers awake in a colossal hollow Rubik-cube structure, with a door in each wall leading to an identical cube. They must find a way out by teamwork, harnessing each other's singular talents (mathematician, criminal, cop, architect, idiot savant, doctor). They must also survive the ingenious, lethal devices that certain cubes are booby-trapped with. And along the way maybe they might find out why they're there. Fiendishly clever sf mystery horror thriller that survives a script with booby traps of its own and some unintentionally hilarious ensemble 'acting' (it often feels like a slightly higher-budget *Blake's* 7 episode). Its labyrinthine set is ingenious (just one cube serves nicely, thank you), and its premise is intriguing, like an sf Kafka Castle.

The Fifth Element [Le Cinquième Elément] (1997, Fr./USA) ★★★★

Dir: Luc Besson; *Prod:* Patrice Ledoux; *Scr:* Besson, Robert Mark Kamen
St: Bruce Willis, Milla Jovovich, Gary Oldman, Ian Holm

Cab driver Korben Dallas' life is a mess, and soon gets messier when beautiful Leeloo literally drops into his hovercab and he is hunted by the police. She is the incarnation of the Fifth Element, the one thing that can combine with the elements of Earth, Air, Fire and Water to defeat the vast force of Evil consuming everything in its path and heading for Earth. The ancient stones of the four elements must be found, but Evil's minion Zorg is also on their trail. Korben and Leeloo must team up to track them down and save the Universe.

Enfant terrible Besson beats Lucas and Spielberg at their own game with humour and wild invention. One of the best-looking sf movies, it was also the most expensive outside Hollywood (nearly $100 million), but made a healthy profit. It's a preposterous camp space opera, an sf cartoon for adults. The atmospheric opening sequence as the Mondoshawans visit Egypt feels like *Raiders Of The Lost Ark* with aliens. The rest resembles a live-action Harry Canyon segment of *Heavy Metal*. Willis is in best action-hero mode, Jovovich is beautiful and suitably alien, and Oldman smoulders with deep-Southern drawl and crazy hairdo. The only downside is diva DJ Ruby Rhod, hammed to the hilt by Chris Tucker, who should have been blown away early. The production design by Dan Weil, costumes by Jean-Paul Gaultier and marvellous CG FX complement Besson's insane vision, originally written when he was at school. Only he could have thought he'd get away with an sf blockbuster called *Zaltman Bleros*, the original name of his lead character!

Men In Black (1997, USA) ★★★

Dir: Barry Sonnenfeld; *Prod:* Laurie MacDonald and Walter F. Parkes; *Scr:* Ed Solomon, based on the comic by Lowell Cunningham
St: Will Smith, Tommy Lee Jones, Linda Fiorentino, Vincent D'Onofrio

Alas Smith and Jones this ain't; the cool comic partnership delivers a fun, intelligent movie for kids and kidults. Basically it's *Ghostbusters* with ETs, as the MIB, New York's FBI department for dealing with real illegal aliens, races against time to stop an intergalactic terrorist assassinating a couple of alien emissaries and stealing a small glass ball containing the entire Universe. Special mention for D'Onofrio's physical turn as a rustic farmer whose body is hijacked by an alien that just won't fit into it. Hugely successful, the inevitable sequel is the inferior *Men In Black II* (2002).

Gattaca (1997, USA) ★★★½

Dir/Scr: Andrew Niccol; *Prod:* Danny De Vito, Michael Shamberg, Stacey Sher
St: Ethan Hawke, Uma Thurman, Jude Law

Back to dystopian society, this time of genetically engineered 'perfect' people versus natural, 'inferior' people. Vincent has the physical and mental potential to achieve his dream of becoming an astronaut, except for the fact that he's natural and therefore cannot. He impersonates the crippled, embittered Jerome to embark on the training programme and falls for the willowy Irene, but when a murder is committed he must somehow stay ahead of the security crackdown.

Intellectual sf with heart and excitement is always welcome, and *Gattaca* is all three. Slightly let down by obvious budget constraints and a shaky performance from Law, it still offered more sf ideas than most of its contemporaries, and furthered a topical debate about genetic selection. Niccol created a splash and immediately followed it with a bigger one as the writer of Peter Weir's huge hit *The Truman Show* (1998), about a man who is unaware that his whole life is a carefully constructed blockbusting reality TV soap. In 2002 he wrote and directed *Simone*, a deft satire about a virtual reality actress who becomes the world's biggest media darling. It did little business and received scant acclaim, but I adore it. It's pin-sharp and very funny, with a great comic turn from the outrageously versatile Al Pacino.

Starship Troopers (1997, USA) ★★★

Dir: Paul Verhoeven; *Prod:* Alan Marshall, Jon Davison; *Scr:* Ed Neumeier
St: Casper Van Dien, Dina Meyer, Denise Richards, Michael Ironside

The film is a giant caricature of nationalism (a point that was largely missed by those who labelled it 'fascistic'), a comic-book version of Heinlein's novel. It ultimately fails not because of suspect politics, but because (a) *Aliens* beat it to the punch and did it better, and (b) its criticisms can convey the opposite message. Like *Robocop*, the satire is sprayed with a fire hose and uses exaggerated ultraviolence to reinforce the absurdity of it all. When the alien Klendathu hurl a ball of fire across space to Earth, taking out hero Johnny Rico's home city of Buenos Aires, the major media debate is about whether or not these bugs are sentient creatures! Verhoeven and Neumeier reprise their earlier message that we need to be more aware of, and immune to, propaganda than ever. Their commercials ('Would You Like To Know More?') echo *Robocop*'s news broadcasts, again questioning the uses to which the media is put by governments. The tragedy is that by making such a trash-aesthetic movie, the satire sails over the teen male audience demographic's collective heads and they'll only get what they came for in the first place: a bug hunt in space.

Open Your Eyes [Abre Los Ojos] (1997, Sp./Fr./It.) ★★★★

Dir: Alejandro Amenábar; *Prod:* Fernando Bovaira, José Luis Cuerda; *Scr:* Amenábar, Mateo Gil
St: Eduardo Noriega, Penélope Cruz, Chete Lera

Either César has a new face after an accident and is in a living hell, or he's dreaming it, or he's in a virtual reality world and his memories are not to be trusted … A demonstration of the difference between Hollywood and art-film narrative, and why the latter should be used much more in sf. *OYE* is a multi-layered, emotionally engaging examination of 'reality' and how perception is a flawed indicator of it. Like *Videodrome* it builds a totally subjective reality, albeit in a less directly sf-nal mode. Cameron Crowe's remake *Vanilla Sky* simplifies the plot and spoonfeeds the meaning to a larger audience. The original is a far better film, and a great example of how ideas can take wing when they're not tenderised into a Hollywood pulp.

Last Night (1998, Can.) ★★★★

Dir/Scr: Don McKellar; *Prod:* Niv Fichman, Daniel Iron
St: McKellar, Sandra Oh, Sarah Polley, David Cronenberg

Last night on Earth; six hours until the End. How and why are unimportant, as is the reason the Sun shines until midnight. What matters is a few ordinary, disparate people living their final precious hours. Patrick is determined to be alone, despite his family's wish for a 'Christmas' celebration. Sandra's efforts to reach husband Duncan are constantly thwarted. Duncan calls his gas company's customers to thank them and wish them well. Craig throws himself into multiple sexual adventures. Jennifer just wants to experience her first. And, relentlessly, the clock ticks down to zero hour. This $2 million movie appeared in the same year as *Armageddon* and is almost its antithesis; an sf character study that supplies its own supercharged ending without CG or pyrotechnics, just old-fashioned emotional truth. Like *On The Beach*, the world is allowed to end not with a bang but with a whimper, and if the studios ever get their collective heads around that melancholic concept they'll make better movies, and *far* better science fiction movies.

The Matrix (1999, USA) ★★★★½

Dir/Scr: Andy and Larry Wachowski; *Prod:* Joel Silver
St: Keanu Reeves, Lawrence Fishburne, Carrie-Anne Moss, Hugo Weaving

Salaryman programmer Thomas Anderson lives a double life. As computer nerd Neo, he's long searched for legendary hacker Morpheus and the secret of the underground myth, The Matrix. After Morpheus' sexy leather-clad sidekick Trinity contacts Neo to say he is in grave danger, he's arrested by secret service Agents and implanted with a live metallic 'bug'. Morpheus rescues him, removes the bug and shows him the unpleasant truth – his life, like everyone else's, is a computer-generated construct. Humanity lies cocooned inside The Matrix, where minds dream 'reality' while bodies are batteries for sentient machines. When an AI became self-aware, the result was nuclear war and the machines now need power to exist on the ravaged planet. Morpheus thinks Neo is 'The One', the new kind of man that can save underground city Zion from the machines and their deadly avatars, the Agents. However, there is a traitor in Morpheus' crew, and fount of all knowledge The Oracle tells Neo that Morpheus is wrong – he is not The One.

The Wachowski brothers ransacked *Star Wars*' narrative and structural philosophy for the first cyberpunk digital myth for adults. After making the superb Hitchcockian thriller *Bound*, they came up with a melange of sf, Hong Kong action cinema, computer games and the Hero's Journey. Innocent hero Neo, like Luke Skywalker, finds the faith to believe in the 'force' within himself and achieve his superhuman potential against the greatest of odds. Although there is a lot of expository dialogue, there is also extraordinary action, choreographed by martial arts expert Yuen Wo-Ping. Complementing the stunts is the spectacular 'bullet-time' special effects photography, allowing the camera to circle around super-slow or frozen moves. *The Matrix*'s appeal to the *X-Files* generation (living a lie, slaves to the machine) is obvious, but its break-out popularity stems from its mythical template. It's derivative but borrows from all the right places. Sure, there's flawed logic (instead of humans, why don't the machines just use electric eels? And why bother feeding their captives a complex mental construct?), but the ambitious nature and marvellous execution of the story more than compensate. Like *SW*, theological elements weave through the text: faith, miracles, resurrection and enlightenment. Add a pot-pourri of popular culture (*Neuromancer, Ghost In The Shell, The Terminator, Alice In Wonderland*) plus Dickian notions of perception/reality, and the result is the best sf thriller in years.

Such a shame that it was undone by its two sequels. While *The Matrix* skilfully navigated skiffy, *The Matrix Reloaded* (2003)★★ and *The Matrix Revolutions* (also 2003) ★★★ became mired in it. Rarely has there been such a gulf between franchise instalments made so close together. *Reloaded* features a woefully misjudged celebration in Zion that reminds me of the turgid Ewoks' dance in *Return Of The Jedi*, and then ties itself in knots with philosophical mumbo-jumbo dialogue that further ruins the pacing. The adult noir/cyberpunk intensity of the first dissipates into action adventure for kids with some great stunts and CG work, but the edge is lost.

eXistenZ (1999, Can./UK) ★★★

Dir/Scr: David Cronenberg; *Prod:* Cronenberg, Andras Hamori, Robert Lantos
St: Jennifer Jason Leigh, Jude Law, Ian Holm, Willem Dafoe

As Seth Brundle says in *The Fly*, 'Is it real, or is it Memorex?' Clever but thin PKD routine from Cronenberg, who was always likely to do Dick, as it were. VR designer Allegra Geller tests her new game eXistenZ with a group of volunteers, each sharing the total experience as the organic game pod is jacked into their spines via an umbycord. When gunmen attempt to kill her and she is rescued by security nerd Ted Pikul, are they on the run or still in the game? It is suitably surreal, with a low-key production design that makes the game environment minimal instead of spectacular, but the scenario never quite works because of this understated look. There's an outright Dick homage in the Perky Pat fast food they eat, a reference to elements within the novel *The Three Stigmata Of Palmer Eldritch*. Leigh dives in and gives her usual reliable performance, but Law struggles to stay afloat. Cronenberg treads water; with any luck he'll one day give us another sf experience to rival *Videodrome*.

2: New Millennium, Old Stories
(2000–2003)

'We are living in ... what Alvin Toffler has labelled blip culture. Toffler has written of our bombardment by these 'short, modular blips of information', but for others the blip is more pervasive and more crucial in its implications. ... the human subject has become a blip: ephemeral, electronically processed, unreal. Numerous writers have noted this implosion, the passage of experiential reality into the grids, matrices and pulses of the electronic information age.'

> Scott Bukatman ('Who Programs You? The Science Fiction of the Spectacle', in *Alien Zone: Cultural Theory and Contemporary Science Fiction Cinema*, ed. Annette Kuhn)

What were we expecting? The end of the world? First contact? An asteroid collision that would extinguish us? The twentieth century became the twenty-first century with over a billion poured into the Millennium Dome in London and assorted worldwide fireworks, but nothing really happened. Nothing *changed*. Everything was familiar, predictable. Then in 2001, although there was no space odyssey, nor anything like it, things really did change. The most sf-nal event of that year, maybe of any year, was the devastating terror attack of September 11 launched on New York and Washington. The world watched, unable to comprehend the horror as hijacked airliners were flown into the World Trade Centre and the Pentagon. In February 2003 the NASA space program was shattered by the destruction of the Shuttle *Columbia*, 17 years after the loss of the *Challenger*. Soon after, the so-called War on Terror saw the US and its allies invade Iraq, a country not responsible for the terror attacks and one that posed no direct threat. Their action metaphorically knocked the world off its axis, and the situation remains balanced on a knife-edge. We are possibly closer to all-out global conflict today than at any time since the early 1960s Cold War stand-off. Many observers have flagged the root cause as the audacious, broad-daylight election coup that 'elected' a dangerous, reactionary right-wing US President in 2000. Perhaps the new millennium did usher in the most seismic change after all. Only time will tell. But this may be a good time to dust off your old sf armageddon movies. *Dr Strangelove* seems more prescient now than ever. And let's try to forget Johnny Smith's momentous handshake with dangerous, reactionary right-wing President Greg Stillson in Cronenberg's/Stephen King's *The Dead Zone* …

The Cell (2000, USA/Ger.) ★★★½

Dir: Tarsem (Singh); *Prod:* Julio Caro, Eric McLeod; *Scr:* Mark Protosevich
St: Jennifer Lopez, Vince Vaughn, Vincent D'Onofrio

Catherine Deane is a social worker recruited by FBI agent Novak to enter the mind of comatose serial killer Carl Stargher in a race to discover where his latest victim is imprisoned before she dies. Catherine then faces a battle to stay alive while being stalked by the killer in the environs of his own diseased mind.

The twisted serial killer plot smokescreens a subversive gothic romance packed with grotesque and disturbing elements. CG never dominates the production design, a lexicon of modern art taking imagery from, amongst others: Giger, Dali, Bacon, Damien Hirst, the Chapman brothers, De Chirico, Picabia, Ernst, Hans Bellmer and M.C. Escher. It lifts mood and imagery from *Seven*, *Silence Of The Lambs* and Jan Svankmajer's animations. *Fantastic Planet* even plays on TV. Pop video director Tarsem's gorgeous-looking film drew much bile, not least a juvenile, offensive and irresponsible personal attack from Harry Knowles' Ain't It Cool News website. The style versus content issue seems to prick people's vitriol glands more than practically any other. Roger Ebert got it about right: 'We live in a time when Hollywood [is] terrified to include anything that might confuse the dullest audience member ... *The Cell* ... is challenging, wildly ambitious and technically superb, and I dunno: I guess it just overloads the circuits for some people ... I know people who hate it, finding it pretentious or unrestrained; I think it's one of the best films of the year.'

Pitch Black (2000, Aust./USA) ★★★

Dir: David Twohy; *Prod:* Tom Engelman; *Scr:* Jim Wheat, Ken Wheat and Twohy
St: Vin Diesel, Radha Mitchell, Cole Hauser

Aliens meets Asimov's *Nightfall* in a tight sf/horror thriller that builds claustrophobic tensions from things that shriek in the dark. A motley crew crashland on a barren desert planet scorched by triple suns, and to stay alive they must repel the nasty denizens of the planet who only come out at night – a long night caused by a rare triple eclipse. Diesel's big break came as dangerous prisoner Riddick, the group's best chance of survival because his eyes have been modified to see in the dark.

Avalon (2001, Jap.) ★★★★

Dir: Mamoru Oshii; *Prod:* Atsushi Kubo; *Scr:* Kazunori Itô
St: Malgorzata Foremniak, Wladyslaw Kowalski, Jerzy Gudejko

In a burned-out world, burned-out people play the VR simulation game Avalon. In their linked state they fight battles against supermachines and try to advance through the game levels. The danger is, if they are killed in the game their minds may not withstand the shock. Ash is a top player, unusually preferring to play alone. She is obsessed with ascending to Class A, where her ex-partner Murphy may or may not be alive.

Oshii couldn't secure full financing in Japan, so moved the production to Poland and shot in the native language. As Kieslowski knew, Poland is a fabulous place to shoot the grimmest of grim realities; in fact, I find this almost a Kieslowskian sf film. The look (bleached-out harsh light and gossamer filters), the ennui, the pacing, the labyrinthine levels of emotion and meaning are augmented by Kenji Kawai's superb quasi-operatic score, reminiscent of Zbigniew Preisner's scores for Kieslowski. *Avalon* is visually breathtaking, and no element more so than the cool beauty of Foremniak. The CG game effects of splintering bodies and tanks, and camera tracks through 2-D reality layers are astounding, but despite their sophistication the wargame scenes are a retroreality harking back to WWII. Murphy isn't the only ghost in this machine, as PKD-style reality conundra arise for characters and audience alike. The top level of Class A is appropriate as the film feels like an ethereal trip, and one you should take.

Minority Report (2002, USA) ★★★

Dir: Steven Spielberg; *Prod:* Jan De Bont, Bonnie Curtis, Gerald R. Molen, Walter F. Parkes; *Scr:* Scott Frank, Jon Cohen, from the story by Philip K. Dick
St: Tom Cruise, Max von Sydow, Colin Farrell, Samantha Morton

Spielberg takes on PKD for the first time and again Dick loses – but much less so than usual; in fact, it may be an honourable draw. This big-budget sf movie looks the part and contains much to recommend. Agonisingly, it's all thrown away at the end (has Spielberg *ever* ended a movie well?) on a resolution that you probably discounted as too stupid and too predictable.

Cypher (2002, USA) ★★★★

Dir: Vincenzo Natali; *Prod:* Paul Federbush, Wendy Grean, Casey La Scala, Hunt Lowry; *Scr:* Brian King
St: Jeremy Northam, Lucy Liu, Nigel Bennett

Meek accountant Morgan Sullivan signs up as a corporate agent for powerful conglomerate Digicorp. Under the alias Jack Thursby he travels to boring cosmetics conferences and transmits them via a concealed recorder. He is racked by intermittent seizures in which he is assailed by lightning-fast, half-glimpsed visions. At a hotel he meets the alluring Rita Foster, who reappears during his next assignment with a bottle of red pills, promising that if he takes them his seizures will cease and he will discover the reality behind his new façade. He finds that the conference delegates are being drugged and hypnotised by Digicorp to believe their cover identities are real. Thanks to the pills he resists the brainwashing, thus becoming a valuable asset to rival company Sunway Systems. They plant him back into Digicorp as a double agent, and supply him with false data. Rita seems to care about Morgan, but she works for mercenary superspy Sebastian Rooks, of whom it is said that to see his face is to die. Morgan is scared, knowing he is a pawn in a deadly three-way chess game. When he delivers the final data disc in person to Sunway's chief technician, his cover is blown. Rita is on hand once more to save his life, but there's something big she's not telling him. And he's finally about to meet Sebastian Rooks ...

Natali followed up his cult hit *Cube* with this spiky techno-espionage thriller, a cross between Hitchcock, Cronenberg and James Bond. The biggest compliment I can pay it is that although it wasn't written by Philip K. Dick, it could have been. *Cypher* is what *Total Recall* was not; a brilliantly directed, razor-sharp kaleidoscope of trademark Dickian obsessions: the shifting nature of identity; problems of perception; different levels of subjective reality; and the manipulation of the individual by external forces. Morgan is plagued by almost patent PKD crises: How do I know what is real or who I am? Can I trust my own senses? Am I being played? If so, by whom and for what purpose? And can I get out of it intact?

The original title was *Company Man*, but Morgan is a *Cypher* in both senses of the word: a secret code and a non-entity. Rita is the key to unlocking his code, but, in order to avoid spoiling an ingenious and well-camouflaged denouement, I'll say no more.

Terminator 3: Rise Of The Machines (2003) ★★½

Dir: Jonathan Mostow; *Prod:* Hal Lieberman, Colin Wilson, Mario F. Kassar, Andrew G. Vajna, Joel B. Michaels; *Scr:* John Brancato and Michael Ferris
St: Arnold Schwarzenegger, Nick Stahl, Claire Danes, Kristanna Loken

A bridge too far for the series, *T3*'s lame finale (if indeed it proves to be) does scant justice to its predecessors. The filmmakers strive to recreate the formula, but succeed only in generating a 2-D caricature; familiarity doesn't quite breed contempt, but certainly great disappointment. Stahl's John Connor is a lightweight leading man, and Arnie's good Terminator shtick is past its sell-by date. The main plus is Loken as the Terminatrix, and the stand-out sequence is one in which she ploughs a crane through LA buildings with Arnie dangling from the jib. Unfortunately, it comes quite early on, and there doesn't seem enough budget left over for the terrible (anti) climax.

1: 2-D Or Beyond 2-D: Animations

Fantastic Planet [La Planète Sauvage] (1973, Fra./Czech.) ★★★

Dir: René Laloux; *Prod:* Roger Corman, Simon Damiani, Anatole Dauman, André Valio-Cavaglione; *Scr:* Laloux, Roland Topor, Steve Hayes, from the novel *Oms en Serie* by Stefan Wul
Voices: Cynthia Adler, Barry Bostwick (English language version)

On the planet Ygam, humanoid Oms are repressed by Draags, giant blue androids. When an Om child, Ter, is 'adopted' as a doll by a Draag child, he becomes educated. After joining the wild Oms he educates them in turn, and leads a rebellion against their Draag tormentors.

This is fantasy, a hypersurreal *Gulliver's Travels*, yet it exerts a more powerful sense of wonder than most sf films by virtue of delirious invention and phenomenal artwork. Even though the Draags and Oms are humanoid, the film ingeniously avoids anthropomorphisation and invents its own set of flora and fauna, some of which leave you laughing with their originality. Laloux shows that there's more to aliens than a few creature workshop suits. You won't find a more densely realised alien environment, or one that matches your wildest, most fevered imaginings of the books you read as a kid. If you could take the weirdness overload, it would make a great double bill with Henson/Oz's *The Dark Crystal* (1982).

Heavy Metal (1981, USA/Can.) ★★★½

Dir: Gerald Potterton; *Prod:* Ivan Reitman; *Scr:* Segment writers inc. Len Blum, Corny Cole, Dan O'Bannon, Angus McKie, Bernie Wrightson, Richard Corben
Voices: John Candy, Roger Bumpass, Eugene Levy, Harold Ramis

Modelled on the eponymous magazine, a US translation/edition of French mag *Metal Hurlant*, famed for its superb artwork and adult-themed material including sex, nudity and violence. These are the start points for the film, a curious mix of sf, horror and fantasy. There are six segments and a clunky framing device based around ownership of evil glowing green sphere the Locnar. The best are *Harry Canyon*, a kind of cyber-punk *Taxi Driver*; Wrightson's hilarious superhero spoof *Captain Sternn*, surely influential to much anime; and the over-long *Taarna*, a fantasy which shouldn't work but does because of its conviction. Also there is *So Beautiful And So Dangerous*, a tale of a couple of stoned pilots, a randy robot and a compliant secretary – a weak segment but the best looking thanks to Angus McKie's artwork; Richard Corben's *Den*, a frankly silly sex fantasy, and *B-17*, O'Bannon's *Twilight Zone*-style horror of a WWII bomber pilot battling his dead crew. Back in 1981 this looked *great* and, despite the adolescent sexism, was a must-see for sf fans. There's also a tremendous score by Elmer Bernstein.

When The Wind Blows (1986, UK) ★★½

Dir: Jimmy T. Murakami; *Prod:* John Coates; *Scr:* Raymond Briggs, from his book
Voices: John Mills, Peggy Ashcroft

Bleak, depressing nuclear drama, which is the point. Jim and Hilda are a naive old English couple caught in the fallout of an atomic blast who bemusedly try to understand and follow survival procedures. A script devoid of dramatic peaks reduces the impact of this worthy attempt to highlight the uselessness of government survival advice (paint your windows, get under your table, etc.). The children's book style of animation goes against the grain of the grim tone, a good idea on paper but one that didn't really work for me. The understatement delivers pathos but feels manipulative. I'd have liked to see Mills and Ashcroft do it for real, and get the message across to a wider audience that if the bomb ever does hit, you and I are doomed.

Akira (1988, Jap.) *****

Dir: Katsuhiro Ôtomo; *Prod:* Shunzu Kato, Ryohei Suzuki; *Scr:* Izou Hashimoto
Voices: Mitsuo Iwata, Nozomu Sasaki

The rebuilt Neo-Tokyo megalopolis stands on the site of the old city, destroyed by nuclear attack in WWIII 30 years before. Punk biker gang leader Kaneda finds himself battling old friend Tetsuo, who has been subjected to government/military mind experiments. Tetsuo's psychokinetic ability is unleashed upon the city as he mutates into an immense, cosmically powerful lifeform. There's also Akira, a frightened child or perhaps a Godlike being, whose own psychic powers may be an evolutionary leap for mankind.

An astonishing assemblage of influences (*Blade Runner*, *2001*, *Judge Dredd* [comic strip not pathetic movie], *Heavy Metal*, cyberpunk and Cronenberg), *Akira* is the yardstick against which anime (Japanimation) is measured. One of the last pre-CG traditional hand-drawn cel animations, its ambition and meticulous technical qualities raise the level of the medium. It offers a revealing lens on a peculiarly Japanese sensibility that sees people merge with machines, and individuals acquire immense powers to trash cities and defeat corrupt state/military might (see also the *Godzilla/Gojira* movies; Shinya Tsukamoto's *Tetsuo: The Iron Man* and *Tetsuo II* [surreal Lynchian fantasies, no relation to Ôtomo's character]; the *Urotsukidoji* series, and RinTaro's *Metropolis*). In the only country to have actually suffered nuclear attack, perhaps this isn't so surprising. Ôtomo adapts his 1,800-page manga (comic) with utmost loving care and attention, and the movie is as fresh and vital as ever. *Akira* seethes with the possibilities of the genre, unrestrained in its energy, colour, scale, violence and headlong flight of imagination. The climactic *2001*-style lightshow spawns a very different Star Child, as the merged entity opens a giant eye and chillingly asserts its psychotic identity: 'I am Tetsuo.' Unmissable.

Ghost In The Shell [Kokaku Kidotai] (1995, Jap.) ★★★★

Dir: Mamoru Oshii; *Prod:* Mitsuhisa Ishikawa, Ken Iyadomi, Yoshimasa Mizuo, Shigeru Watanabe; *Scr:* Kazunori Ito, from the manga by Masamune Shirow
Voices: Atsuko Tanaka, Akio Otsuka

A resourceful hacker known as the Puppet Master is accessing government operatives. Special Forces Section 6 is on his case, in the persons of Bateau and Major Kusanagi, who has had her human body replaced with a cyborg one. Each time they think they have him, it's another blind alley. Finally, the Puppet Master chooses his moment to reveal his identity: a powerful, complex government software program that has achieved AI status.

One of the densest, most thoughtful and believable sf worlds ever created, even if Oshii's breast fetish does move uncomfortably close to *Heavy Metal*. The creation of a new lifeform (a merging of Kusanagi and the AI) is a more optimistic slant on *Akira*. As he would in *Avalon*, Oshii showed he is not afraid to run with and expand upon philosophical themes of intelligence, responsibility, identity and alienation. Where is the religious concept of a soul left if memory is fully externalised and requires no body to sustain it? If one can hack computers, will we not also be able to hack/control cyborgs? If lifeforms can merge, what is the limit? (and I discount merged entities like V'ger/Ilia/Decker in *ST:TMP* etc. because the writers don't care). The 'Through a glass darkly' verse from Corinthians is used well to illustrate the context. Such melancholy is unusual for Western sf, with rare exceptions like *Blade Runner*. Visually, *GITS* is lavish and stunning, and had a profound influence on the Wachowski brothers.

The Iron Giant (1999, USA) ★★★★

Dir: Brad Bird; *Prod:* Allison Abbate, Des McAnuff; *Scr:* Bird, Tim McCanlies, from the book *The Iron Man* by Ted Hughes
Voices: Jennifer Aniston, Harry Connick, Jr, Vin Diesel

Rockwell, Maine, the 1950s. Young Hogarth Hughes is exploring the woods when he sees a giant robot, many storeys tall, caught in live power station wires. He manages to pull the master lever and saves its life. The robot is friendly, but has no memory of its origin or purpose after crash landing on Earth. It eats iron – a *lot* of iron – so where better to hide it than in beatnik junk sculptor Dean's scrapyard. However, the Feds are not far behind and scuzzball spook Kent is onto Hogarth. When Kent finds his proof he calls in the military but their weapons are useless. Under attack, the robot reverts to its programming as a superweapon until Hogarth prevents it from destroying the soldiers. The General observes the robot's conscience and friendship with the boy, but Kent grabs his radio and orders a nuclear attack. Rockwell awaits its fate, but the robot flies into orbit to take the full force of the warhead's explosion outside the atmosphere. The grateful townspeople commission Dean to make a memorial sculpture of the Iron Giant. Meanwhile on an icy glacier, the robot's beacon flashes atop its head, calling its scattered parts back together.

An affectionate homage to 50s sf films, *The Iron Giant* looks gorgeous in a semi-Miyazake style, and boasts an excellent script that masterfully builds the viewer's empathy for the robot. Once again, the Federal government's policy is to shoot first and ask questions later, destroying what it doesn't understand. The subtext delivers a resonant Cold War parable: Hogarth teaches the robot that being a weapon is a matter of choice, not programming. It's a fast-paced, confident film, as much for adults as children, and the climax is a *real* tear-jerker.

Warners' disastrous marketing campaign prompted a media outcry including editorials in prominent US newspapers asking why they were letting a great movie die. Harry Knowles raved: 'This is the first film I have seen that has honestly learned everything you should take from *E.T.* ... but then improved on every single point.'

Final Fantasy: The Spirits Within
(2001, Jap./USA) ★★★★

Dir: Hironobu Sakaguchi, Motonori Sakakibara; *Prod:* Jun Aida, Chris Lee, Akio Sakai; *Scr:* Sakaguchi, Al Reinert, Jeff Vintar, Jack Fletcher
Voices: Ming-Na, Alec Baldwin, Ving Rhames, James Woods

2065. It is 34 years since a meteor strike in the Caspian mountains unleashed hordes of diaphanous aliens whose very touch is lethal. Humanity now lives in fortified enclaves and is trying to reclaim the Earth. Dr Aki Ross and her mentor Dr Sid are searching for the final two of eight kinds of spirit DNA that, when combined, will negate the aliens' lifeforce. General Hein doesn't believe in such mumbo-jumbo and has built Zeus, a gigantic orbital laser weapon, to obliterate the aliens at source – the impact crater. Dr Sid claims that firing Zeus could kill Gaia, the Earth spirit. The council gives Aki a short time to complete her research, chaperoned by a military unit led by old flame Gray. Will it be enough, or will Hein force his own deadly agenda? Can the alien DNA within Aki remain contained or will it consume her? And will her telepathic 'dreams' of a cataclysmic war on an alien planet supply the answers she seeks?

Final Fantasy is a genuine landmark: the first CGI film to attempt to create realistic human characters. Using an arsenal of sophisticated gadgetry, including state-of-the-art 3-D motion-capture software, at times it's so effective that you forget you're watching animation. After a preview at the impressive Sony Imageworks theatre in LA I was awed and elated, my childhood sense of wonder and fascination with sf movie visual effects elevated to its greatest extent in years. There are caveats, though: the plot's Haight-Ashbury mysticism is overcooked; the characters are just as stereotypical as in 'real' Hollywood sf; and on a couple of occasions the animation resembles the computer game it's taken from. However, plusses far outweigh minuses, and it is required viewing for its amazing spectacle. The opening sequence, as Aki searches for a single plant at night in the ruins of Times Square, is one of several flawless combinations of design, suspense and action. A unique and scandalously underappreciated achievement, *FF* is yet another victim of the studios' painful inability to market complex sf to a wide audience. In its opening week it took $11 million; in the same week Burton's *Planet Of The Apes* took nearly $70 million. Enough said.

0: ZEROS: Exploded On The Launch Pad

'Greetings my friends. We are all interested in the future, for that is where you and I are going to spend the rest of our lives. And remember my friends, future events such as these will affect you, in the future. You are interested in the unknown, the mysterious, the unexplainable — that is why you are here. And now, for the first time, we are bringing you the full story of what happened on that fateful day. We are giving you all the evidence, based only on the secret testimony of the miserable souls who survived this terrifying ordeal. The incidents, the places — my friends, we cannot keep this a secret any longer … My friends, can your hearts stand the shocking facts about grave robbers from outer space..?'

Criswell (Fake psychic, narrator of *Plan 9 From Outer Space*, I swear I'm not making this up …)

Robot Monster (1953, USA)

Dir/Prod: Phil Tucker; *Scr:* Wyatt Ordung
St: George Barrows, Gregory Moffett, George Nader

Robot monster = man in large gorilla suit with diving helmet for head. Need I say more?

Plan 9 From Outer Space (1956, USA)

Dir/Prod/Scr: Edward D. Wood, Jr
St: Gregory Walcott, Mona McKinnon, Bela Lugosi, Criswell

The most famous failure of all time, elevated to the cream of the bottom of the barrel by Michael and Harry Medved's infamous

Golden Turkey Awards which renewed interest in the film and the 'career' of its eccentric director Wood. *Plan 9* is so gloriously awful that it should be studied as a singular genre; one in which coherence, logic, in fact anything to do with reality is not only unnecessary but undesirable. See it with a bunch of friends and several beers, when it becomes one of the funniest comedies ever. Also don't miss Tim Burton's loving biopic *Ed Wood*, one of the best films about a filmmaker ever made.

Zardoz (1973, UK)

Dir/Prod/Scr: John Boorman
St: Sean Connery, Charlotte Rampling, Sara Kestelman

'The gun is good! The penis is evil!' Boorman made *Point Blank* (1967), a great thriller and *Excalibur* (1981), a visually extravagant retelling of the Arthurian legend. But he also made *Exorcist II: The Heretic*, one of the worst celluloid atrocities. And *Zardoz* ... Somewhere in here is an interesting allegory about control of the masses by the privileged elite and the lies they propagate as truth, but it's buried under extreme pretention, embarrassing dialogue and an amateur dramatic/Monty Python tone. Connery runs around in a red nappy turning on bare-breasted women (immortal males can't get erect), while the 60s trip continues with a giant stone flying head and multiple symbolic references (the wiZARD of OZ, man). Admirable in its aim of uniting dystopian sf and Swiftian satire, but nowhere near up to the task, it's worth a look if you want a one-off, anti-Hollywood sf film and you've plenty of spare drugs.

Logan's Run (1976, USA)

Dir: Michael Anderson; *Prod:* Saul David; *Scr:* David Zelag Goodman, from the novel by William F. Nolan and George Clayton Johnson
St: Michael York, Jenny Agutter, Richard Jordan, Roscoe Lee Browne

The youth of tomorrow live inside a big dome, do nothing until their thirtieth birthdays, then float around inside the carousel and go to a better life. Actually, they die, but they don't know that. A canny few figure it for a con and run. These 'runners' are hunted by Sandmen and 'retired'. Logan is a Sandman who goes undercover to try to find 'Sanctuary', the mythical place where the runners are headed. He and arm candy Jessica discover that the outside is habitable, and bring back old man Ballard (Peter Ustinov paying for his kitchen extension) to show the people in the dome that life doesn't have to end at 30 and everything they believed is wrong. Logan blows up the computer, giving freedom to all.

If you write a good sf novel, beware. The better it is, the more likely Hollywood is to fuck it up. The true crime here is against the authors, who didn't deserve to have Saul David or Michael Anderson foisted upon their work. Anderson has a solid sf track record; he's destroyed everything he's touched. He ruined John Varley's excellent *Millennium*, wrecked Ray Bradbury's classic *Martian Chronicles* on TV and, as far back as 1956, reduced Orwell's seminal *1984* to a lumbering snooze-fest. At least the principle that only the worst movies should be remade is being upheld by Bryan Singer (*The Usual Suspects, X-Men*), who is doing just that.

The Black Hole (1979, USA)

Dir: Gary Nelson; *Prod:* Ron Miller; *Scr:* Jeb Rosebrook, Gerry Day
St: Maximilian Schell, Anthony Perkins, Robert Forster, Yvette Mimieux

Disney's megabuck summer blockbuster was so bad it created its own singularity and disappeared straight into it. This is kiddie fare by design and definition, but it's also loathsome rubbish, one of the films I've come closest to walking out of (you'll no doubt be proud that I've never yet done so, not even *Fatal Attraction*).

Flash Gordon (1980, UK)

Dir: Mike Hodges; *Prod:* Dino De Laurentiis; *Scr:* Lorenzo Semple, Jr
St: Sam J. Jones, Melody Anderson, Max Von Sydow, Ornella Muti

This swollen fantasy fruitbowl marks a low point in Von Sydow's long career and assaulted our ears with Brit pomp-rock band Queen's nauseating score. Hodges, director of superb, gritty UK thriller *Get Carter* (1971), was an odd choice to helm. Scripted by Semple, Jr (responsible for the original camp crusading *Batman* movie), one can only assume that it was *meant* to be like this. Hodges turned his hand to sf once more, with the 'comedy' *Morons From Outer Space* (1985). On second thoughts, come back Flash, all is forgiven.

Inseminoid [aka Horror Planet] (1981, UK)

Dir: Norman J. Warren; *Prod:* Richard Gordon, David Speechley; *Scr:* Gloria Maley, Nick Maley
St: Robin Clarke, Judy Geeson, Stephanie Beacham

Shameless no-budget rip-off of *Alien*, with a cast of Brit nobodies menaced by a, well, an alien lifeform with a penchant for inseminating Earth women. And even if you're the kind of person for whom that might sound interesting, please believe me – it isn't.

Waterworld (1995, USA)

Dir: Kevin Reynolds; *Prod:* Charles Gordon, John A. Davis, Kevin Costner; *Scr:* Peter Rader, David N. Twohy, Joss Whedon
St: Costner, Jeanne Tripplehorn, Dennis Hopper

Legendarily profligate with a $200 million spend, *Waterworld* (or, Mad Max On The Ocean Wave) was bedevilled by Kong-size problems: the hyper-expensive set sank and had to be rebuilt, and infighting between director and star allegedly culminated in Costner locking Reynolds out of the editing room. Amazingly, the film was rescued by an astute publicity strategy that exaggerated its already gargantuan woes. The scuttlebutt that it was so out of control and such a stinking pile drew many people along to rubberneck, including me, and it eventually broke even! Go see the Waterworld event at Universal Studios instead, it's a lot more exciting.

Screamers (1995, Can./USA/Jap.)

Dir: Christian Duguay; *Prod:* Franco Battista, Tom Berry; *Scr:* Dan O'Bannon, Miguel Tejada-Flores, from the short story *Second Variety* by Philip K. Dick
St: Peter Weller, Roy Dupuis, Jennifer Rubin

Wondersubstance Berynium has been found on Sirius-6, sparking a war for control between the mining company and Earth Alliance. No-man's land is seeded with buried self-replicating robot assassins, Screamers, which dissect anyone not wearing an Alliance electronic armband. An Alliance Commander and a recent arrival from a crashlanded transporter set off for a pow-wow at the mining HQ. En route they find that the Screamers are making Davids; lethal robots that look like small boys with teddy bears, and the mining HQ has been overrun by them. Weller and a small band of survivors trek back to the Alliance base, where guess what's happened?

A good thing that PKD didn't live to see his metaphysical short drenched in testosterone and moulded into industrial waste. A few gems: an Alliance General is revealed as a hologram, after an automatic door has just opened for him! Weller sets off across the wasteland, not with his deputy but with an idiot he's just met, who may even have been a prisoner. Now that's trust! Said idiot wears a *Walkman* and can't hear danger! They meet a small boy (one of the Davids, of course), and allow him to tag along despite his lack of armband, which means he should be shredded in seconds (and when he isn't, should start ringing major alarm bells). The armbands stop the Screamers attacking Weller's group, but the Alliance base personnel also wear them, yet they are all killed. The end supplies one of the most brain-freezing denouements ever, as a Screamer learns to love (aaah!), topped by a final shot that defies belief. O'Bannon proves a paycheck's a paycheck and PKD gets shafted again.

Independence Day [aka ID4] (1996, USA)

Dir: Roland Emmerich; *Prod:* Dean Devlin; *Scr:* Devlin, Emmerich
St: Will Smith, Bill Pullman, Jeff Goldblum, Robert Loggia

Effects don't make a movie, but the sense of wonder established by the arrival of the giant alien ships is memorable. Unfortunately, the film then descends into jingoistic masturbation as a wisecracking airforce hero with a stripper girlfriend teams up with Goldblum's patented nerd to sabotage the aliens with a computer virus (after *War Of The Worlds'* biological virus) and save the day. The President's wife dies (boo!), but that's okay because he gets to become a war hero again (yaay!) and the US kicks alien butt on 4th July (awlright!).

Emmerich trashes New York, as he did in *Godzilla* and *The Day After Tomorrow*. *ID4* grossed over £300 million, so he could do what he liked. Almost every plot event gets the electric chair from the court of logic. A couple of the best: the nerd takes down the alien computers with a Mac laptop, a neat trick as they don't interface with anything on Earth. The jock and the nerd gain entry to the alien mothership in the 50-year-old Roswell saucer, akin to going up in a Winnebago, but the aliens don't notice – they may as well be in a black sphere with 'BOMB' painted on the side. Go to http://www.imdb.com/title/tt0116629/board/nest/8919660 for a full list of howlers.

Event Horizon (1997, USA)

Dir: Paul W.S. Anderson; *Prod:* Jeremy Bolt, Lawrence Gordon, Lloyd Levin; *Scr:* Philip Eisner
St: Lawrence Fishburne, Sam Neill, Kathleen Quinlan, Joely Richardson

A mission discovers the eponymous ship, we're told in a decaying orbit around Neptune, but it's actually inside the planet's atmosphere! This is the scientific level we're at. The ship's revolutionary drive has the side-effect of opening a gateway into hell, where really BAD things happen, and inventor Dr Weir(d) will do anything to protect his baby. Trouble is, he's Sam Neill. Yep, cuddly Sam Neill, who, even with his eyes gouged out, is about as menacing as Roger Rabbit. Unashamedly *Hellraiser* in space, young girls'll wet themselves and young guys'll think it *rocks*, but the rest of us should find it derivative, poorly acted and predictable. Hint: the name Paul W.S. Anderson on the poster or trailer is as good a warning not to see a movie as there is. For further proof, watch *Soldier* or *Alien Vs. Predator*, tag line 'Whoever wins, we lose.' Never a truer word …

Lost In Space (1998, USA)

Dir: Stephen Hopkins; *Prod:* Mark W. Koch, Hopkins, Akiva Goldsman, Carla Fry; *Scr:* Goldsman
St: William Hurt, Gary Oldman, Matt LeBlanc, Heather Graham

LIS monopolised the VFX industry in London and, in summer 1998, crew screenings took place in the 1,000-seat Empire cinema in Leicester Square. I attended with a friend, who, like his fellow digital FX artists, had bust a gut to meet the deadline. The response was a stunned, tomblike silence; the effects looked pretty good, but the movie *stank*. It was a strange experience to sit among an audience radiating tangible waves of hatred and disappointment towards the end product of two years of their lives. It was just so *wrong* in every respect. It works neither as a homage to the 60s TV series, nor, unless you're under five, as science fiction. The cynical corporate studio attitude is personified by the Blawp, a Godawful weird/cute alien shoehorned into the movie for no reason whatsoever except to shift merchandise.

Battlefield: Earth (2000, USA)

Dir: Roger Christian; *Prod:* Jonathan D. Krane, Elie Samaha, John Travolta; *Scr:* Corey Mandell and J.D. Shapiro, from the novel by L. Ron Hubbard
St: Travolta, Barry Pepper, Forest Whitaker

Hubbard was kind of the Arthur Hailey of sf, but his chief legacy to the world isn't his writing, it's Dianetics/Scientology, a 'religion' that could only have been made in America, and with about as much defining intellectual thrust as the Force. Hollywood, home to some of the wealthiest but most insecure people in the world, has many adherents. Their detached view from the top of the capitalist pile is that they must be right. Wrong! Travolta, one such adherent, undid his resurrection in *Pulp Fiction* by following his leader, piloting his mega-potboiler right into the Sun. It wins a special Academy Award for its achievement of reaching the bottom of the barrel and proving the existence of an infinity of barrels which it then endlessly plummets through. Travolta's character Terl's most potent curse is 'rat-brain', a term that grossly flatters the collective intelligence of those responsible for this atrocity.

Mission To Mars (2000, USA)

Dir: Brian De Palma; *Prod:* Tom Jacobson; *Scr:* Jim Thomas, John Thomas, Graham Yost
St: Tim Robbins, Gary Sinise, Don Cheadle, Connie Nielsen

Insulting Z-movie scenario with pretentions to *2001* gravitas. Like *ID4* It's unpalatably all-American, like being force-fed a truckload of burgers, Mom's apple pie and gallons of chocolate malt. The characters are cutouts. The script tells us everything three times to make sure we get it. Sinise wears enough eyeliner for a John Hughes New Romantic movie. Morricone's score is so intrusive it feels like a musical. Product placement is everywhere: *Dr Pepper's Mission To Mars*. The story ...? After a looong build-up the crew reach Mars, discover that the land formation vaguely resembling a face is ... a face, an artefact left as a sign by Martians who fled across the Universe after a huge asteroid collision, which was odd given the perfectly habitable planet next door. The face is booby-trapped, which is idiotic; it's like Voyager's message of greetings from the people of Earth hiding a nuclear bomb. *M2M* is, as many have pointed out, an ideal candidate for *Mystery Science Theater 3000*.

Ghosts Of Mars (2001, USA)

Dir: John Carpenter; *Prod:* Sandy King; *Scr:* Larry Sulkis, Carpenter
St: Natasha Henstridge, Ice Cube, Joanna Cassidy, Jason Statham

There's little point dignifying this with a synopsis. Carpenter's long tailspin has been like watching a man running towards a clifftop on frame advance, and it seems he's beyond repair. I hope I'm wrong, remembering *Dark Star*, *Assault On Precinct 13*, *Halloween* and *The Thing* ... but then there's *Memoirs Of An Invisible Man*, *Village Of The Damned*, *Escape From LA* ... I'd find it difficult to believe it's the same man were it not for my encounters with him at the San Diego Comic-Con. He looks like he'd rather be elsewhere and often gets *very* tetchy when answering questions. His demeanour suggests that he is aware of his current predicament but can't beat it. It must be galling to have to watch populist hacks like Roland Emmerich sweep in and conquer Hollywood, but that doesn't excuse his own train wrecks. I humbly suggest he goes back to his roots: low budgets and taut, suspenseful scripts where he can hopefully rediscover his immense talent and rebuild his reputation.

Planet Of The Apes (2001, USA)

Dir: Tim Burton; *Prod:* Richard D. Zanuck; *Scr:* William Broyles, Jr, Lawrence Conner, Mark D. Rosenthal
St: Mark Wahlberg, Tim Roth, Helena Bonham Carter, Michael Clarke Duncan

None of Burton's trademark flair is evident in this inept 'reimagining'. I sat through this and *Ghosts Of Mars* in the same weekend; more torture than mortal man should bear. It's packed with enough skiffy for ten Ed Wood movies; as Roger Ebert said, 'Science fiction for junior high-school boys.'

A selection: the apes are afraid of water and they have no boats. So how did they build reservoirs or plumb their homes? One ape can kill another bare-handed in seconds, yet the strongest of them barely scratches Wahlberg in two minutes. A gazillion of them, armed to the teeth, are held off by a handful of far slower, far weaker humans. Wahlberg finds a long-demolished spaceship, and whaddyaknow? It not only works at the touch of a button but it still has fuel! Con-veen-ient! Woody Allen starting a 200-year-old VW Beetle in *Sleeper* was more believable. *Then* the monkey, long since discarded by the 'plot', arrives in the ship, defying incalculable odds. Which are chicken feed compared to Wahlberg chancing upon the space/time co-ordinates to get back to – where? – and landing safely. On a planet with an evolved gorilla race that can land-scape water features, lakes and fountains, and design buildings that are Earth circa now, complete with recognisable land-marks, and are *far too small* for them! Just like the police cars …

Mainstream Hollywood ceased giving a monkey's about sf a long time ago. In truth, we deserve it, because we made it a hit, but this and *Ghosts Of Mars* and *Mission To Mars* and *Hollow Man* and *What Lies Beneath* and several others in a year was way too much. If Kubrick could have foreseen the cinematic dreck of 2001, he'd probably have blown the Earth to smithereens at the end of his odyssey.

A.I. Artificial Intelligence (2001, USA)

Dir: Steven Spielberg; *Prod:* Spielberg, Bonnie Curtis, Kathleen Kennedy; *Scr:* Spielberg, based on a screen story by Ian Watson, from the story *Supertoys Last All Summer Long* by Brian Aldiss
St: Haley Joel Osment, Jude Law, Frances O'Connor, Brendan Gleeson

Another communiqué from the kindergarten. Spielberg took the reins of Kubrick's project after his death and for the opening 20 minutes or so, I was duped into thinking that maybe at last he had come up with a powerful, adult sf hybrid. Soon after, when the artificial boy is abandoned in the forest, I got a 'bad feeling about this'. Two hours later (though it seemed like ten) it had curdled into *Pinocchio*, with Disney syrup and multiple bogus endings. I mourned Kubrick's passing all the more: compare Spielberg's juvenile 'Barnum and Bailey' Flesh Fair sequence with the tension and menace that the master would have given us. *A.I.* – Anti Intelligence.

−1: Afterword: The New Dystopia?

'Man is the only creature aware of his own mortality and is at the same time generally incapable of coming to terms with this awareness and all its implications.'

Stanley Kubrick (writer/director)

'Futuristic science fiction tends to be pessimistic … Someone once said something I believe is true: if you live in the past, you're depressed and if you live in the future, you're anxious, so the only way to feel okay is to live in the present.'

Michael Crichton (writer/director)

In the post–2001 landscape, sf films continue to rely on CG spectacle because studios' ideas are scarce as oil in Mad Max's desert. But we don't need a post-apocalyptic world to find science fiction, because it's already here. Most of us in the blip culture live in middle-class safety, where cultural values, morals, ethics and justice are fixed concepts, applied to all. And if you believe that, you'll believe in UFOs. Wells and Verne would consider our world a pure dystopia; an overcrowded place of insane chaos and terrifying flux.

Two World Wars, the Cold War, Vietnam, Kosovo, Iraq, China, Afghanistan, Rwanda, Chechnya, Palestine, Northern Ireland, Algeria, North/South Korea, India and Pakistan, extreme nationalistic and fundamentalist violence; governments pursuing covert agendas; politicians smilingly telling us black is white; the daily suffering and hardship of millions of living, breathing human beings … If you're well situated within the capitalist economy you probably consider life idyllic, but it's an idyll built on quicksand; a tailored Stepford lie. A luxury yacht won't sail the tide of hatred, intolerance and conflict enveloping us once again.

The individual is more expendable and at the mercy of insidious control mechanisms than ever before. Everything can be spun or crushed: personality, identity, belief, purpose, cause. The media, especially television, is complicit in this process, exploited by governmental and corporate interests (essentially similar) for political and ideological programming. Big Brother dominates people's lives via a sprawling network of propaganda as the system resists any other system outside itself. We OBEY and CONSUME, we won't wear the glasses, we don't question the Matrix, because the more we have to think about *real* collective reality, the more we're forced to confront its awful nature. And the more we do that, the more our consciences might shout at us to do something. 'Reality' is a PKD/*Videodrome* dystopian construct, with torpor at its core, to keep the *Starship Troopers* horrors at bay.

But sf technology also offers a way to combat Big Brother – through the Internet. The World Wide Web proves William Gibson's assertion that information wants to be free; free from repression, censorship and misrepresentation. And while it remains at liberty, it's our best hope of avoiding what I hope is not our programmed destiny, to repeat the disastrous mistakes of history. But where will change arise if not from you and I and millions like us? Recent global terrorism and US/coalition activities suggest that some of the harshest sf dystopias may be more predictive and less asinine than we suspected. We may yet receive a visit from a galactic emissary like Klaatu giving us a simple ultimatum to mend our ways or face annihilation.

Or, even more unthinkably, we may not.

References And Notes

Books On Science Fiction Films:

A Distant Technology: Science Fiction Film And The Machine Age by J.P. Telotte, US: Wesleyan University Press, 1999, Paperback, 218pp, ISBN 0819563463

Alien Zone: Cultural Theory And Contemporary Science Fiction Cinema ed. Annette Kuhn, UK/US Verso, 1990, Paperback, 231pp, ISBN 0860919935

An Illustrated History Of Horror And Science Fiction Films by Carlos Clarens, US: Da Capo, 1997, Paperback, 328pp, ISBN 0306808005

A Pictorial History Of Science Fiction Films by Jeff Rovin, US: Citadel Press, 1975, Paperback, 240pp, ISBN 0806505370 (O.O.P.)

Fantastic Cinema by Peter Nicholls, UK: Ebury Press, 1984, Paperback, 224pp, £6.95, ISBN 0852233477 (O.O.P.)

Future Tense: The Cinema Of Science Fiction by John Brosnan, UK: Macdonald and Jane's, 1978, Hardback, 320pp, ISBN 035404222X (O.O.P.)

Keep Watching The Skies! American Science Fiction Movies Of The Fifties, Volume I 1950–1957 by Bill Warren, US: McFarland & Co. Inc., 1982, Hardback, 467pp, ISBN 0899500323 (O.O.P.)

Keep Watching The Skies! American Science Fiction Movies Of The Fifties, Volume II 1958–1962 by Bill Warren, US: McFarland & Co. Inc., 1986, Hardback, 839pp, ISBN 0899501702 (O.O.P.)

Omni's Screen Flights/Screen Fantasies:The Future According To Science Fiction Cinema, ed. Danny Peary, US: Doubleday, 1984, Paperback, 310pp, ISBN 0385192029 (O.O.P.)

Replications: A Robotic History Of The Science Fiction Film by J.P. Telotte, US: University Of Illinois Press, 1995, Paperback, 222pp, ISBN 0252064666

Science Fiction/Horror: A Sight And Sound Reader ed. Kim Newman, UK: BFI, 2002, Paperback, 325pp, ISBN 0851708978

Science Fiction: Studies In Film by Frederik Pohl and Frederik Pohl IV, US: Ace, 1981, Paperback, 346pp, No ISBN given (O.O.P.)

Science Fiction Movies by Philip Strick, UK: Octopus, 1976, Hardback, 160pp, ISBN 070640470X (O.O.P.)

Screening Space: The American Science Fiction Film (2nd ed.) by Vivian Sobchack, US: Rutgers University Press, 1997, Paperback, 345pp, ISBN 081352492X

The Primal Screen: A History Of Science Fiction Film by John Brosnan, UK: Orbit, 1991, Hardback, 402pp, ISBN 0356202224

Other Books Of Interest:

Cult Movies by Danny Peary, UK: Vermilion, 1982, Paperback, 402pp, ISBN 0091506018

Cult Movies 2 by Danny Peary, US: Dell, 1983, Paperback, 181pp, ISBN 0440516323

Cult Movies 3 by Danny Peary, US: Simon & Schuster, 1988, Paperback, 286pp, ISBN 0671648101

The Encyclopedia Of Science Fiction by John Clute and Peter Nicholls, UK: Orbit, 1993, Hardback, 1,370pp, ISBN 1857231244

Science Fiction Film Magazines:

Cinefantastique: http://www.cfq.com – has lost much of its edge but in its heyday *the* best sf movie mag, with exceptional content and images, often devoting double issues to in-depth features on single films. Back issues are available from its inception in 1970 onwards. Early volumes have excellent features on pre-1970 sf movies and are fairly pricey.

Cinefex: http://www.cinefex.com/home.html – technical, nuts-and-bolts glossy SPFX mag with superb features and images. Again, you can obtain back issues from the site, dating from the early 80s. The first dozen or so issues are sold out and tend to be very expensive.

Starburst: http://www.visimag.com/starburst/ – more lightweight than CFQ and Cinefex, but a useful chronicler of sf and fantasy movies since the late 70s. Back issues are available from the mid-80s.

Starlog: http://www.starlog.com – UK mag also active since the late 70s, similar in approach and quality to *Starburst*.

Science Fiction Film Websites:

http://hubcap.clemson.edu/~sparks/sffilm/linksfilm.html
http://www.filmsite.org/sci-fifilms.html
http://www.magicdragon.com/UltimateSF/SF-Index.html
http://www.lib.berkeley.edu/MRC/Scififilm.html
http://www.moria.co.nz/sf

http://www.suite101.com/subjectheadings/contents.cfm/310
http://www.umich.edu/~umfandsf/film/films/

Individual Film/Director Websites:

http://classics.www5.50megs.com/gort/index.htm (*The Day The Earth Stood Still*)

http://scribble.com/uwi/br/off-world.html (*Blade Runner*)

http://www.bmonster.com/index.html (Monster and Cult movies)

http://www.fortunecity.com/lavendar/sydenham/306/rid.html (Ridley Scott)

http://www.geocities.com/Area51/4456/thx1138.html (*THX 1138*)

http://www.krusch.com/kubrick/kq.html (Stanley Kubrick)

http://www.starwars.com/ (I forget what this one's about …)

http://wso.williams.edu/~mhacker/clockwork.html (*A Clockwork Orange*)

http://wso.williams.edu/~mhacker/strangelove2.html (*Dr. Strangelove*)

http://www.wsu.edu/~brians/science_fiction/terminator.html (*The Terminator*)

Other Websites:

http://www.aint-it-cool-news.com – Harry Knowles' legendary geek-site gives the scuttlebutt first on upcoming films. Warning: although fun, these are often the barely edited ravings of a bunch of American adolescents. If you want academic opinions much beyond 'It kicked ASS!' or 'Maan, this SUCKS!', try some of the above books, mags and sites first.

http://www.imdb.com – information/comments about any movie, sf or otherwise.